Writer's Workbook

Level 5

Annotated Teacher's Edition

A Division of The McGraw·Hill Companies

Columbus, Ohio

www.sra4kids.com

SRA/McGraw-Hill

A Division of The McGraw·Hill Companies

Copyright ©2002 by SRA/McGraw-Hill

Send all inquiries to:
SRA/McGraw-Hill
8787 Orion Place
Columbus, OH 43240-4027

Printed in the United States of America

ISBN 0-07-569556-1

 2 3 4 5 6 7 8 9 QPD 06 05 04 03 02

Table of Contents

Unit 4   Making a New Nation
Persuasive Writing

Unit 5   Going West
Personal Writing

Unit 6   Journeys and Quests

Narrative Writing

Cumulative Checklists

Name _____ Date _____

Autobiography

Objective: Students prewrite for an autobiography.

Use the writing process to write an autobiography.

Prewriting

Who is the audience for your autobiography?

☐ Your teacher

☐ Your class

☐ Your family

☐ A friend

☐ Other **Audience should be specific.**

What is your purpose for writing your autobiography?

☐ You want to inform your audience about your life history and describe how key events influenced who you are.

☐ You want to entertain your audience by telling about interesting, funny, and exciting things that happened to you throughout your life.

☐ Other **Purpose should be clearly stated.**

Autobiography • **Writer's Workbook**

UNIT I Cooperation and Competition • **Lesson 3** *Juggling*

▶ Autobiography

Objective: Students plan an autobiography using a chain-of-events chart.

THE WRITITNG PROCESS

Plan the ideas for your autobiography. Fill in the chain-of-events chart with key life events. The first box should list your birth. Have students list events. They do not need to use complete sentences.

Main Idea _____

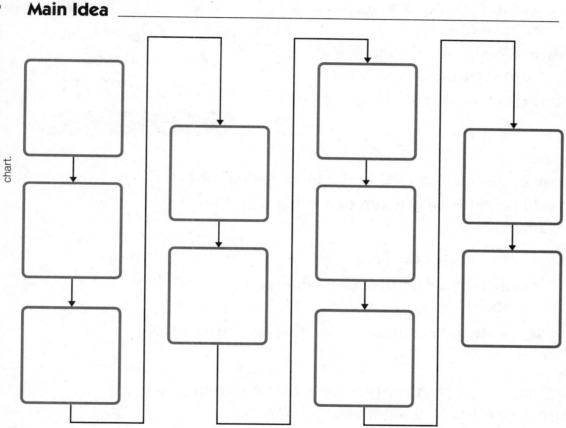

Plan the details of your autobiography. Add exact or approximate dates to your time line. Add any details about the events.

Drafting

Write the first draft of your autobiography on a sheet of paper. Try to turn each life event into a paragraph.

Name _____ Date _____

▶ **Autobiography**

Revising

Read through your autobiography. Use this checklist to pinpoint areas for improvement. Use proofreading marks to make changes.

Proofreading Marks

∧	Add something.
℮	Take something out.
⊂⊃	Close up space.
#	Add space.
⊙	Add a period.

Ideas

☐ Does your autobiography develop events logically around a theme?

☐ Do you provide interesting details and examples from your life?

☐ Can your audience easily understand your ideas?

Organization

☐ Are sentences and paragraphs in the most logical order?

☐ Can you add or improve transitions so that they better guide the reader?

Word Choice and Sentence Fluency

☐ Are there words that better describe what you thought or felt about events?

☐ Did you vary sentence beginnings, lengths, and structures?

Voice

☐ Imagine your readers as they read your autobiography. Is your writing targeted to your specific audience?

☐ Could your writing be changed to show more enthusiasm and a willingness to share who you are and how events shaped you?

☐ Other **Answers may include any items specific to autobiographies.**

Make all of your changes on your draft. Add anything else that will improve your autobiography.

Objective: Students edit/proofread and publish an autobiography.

▶ **Autobiography**

Editing/Proofreading

Carefully proofread your autobiography. After having spent the time to plan, draft, and revise your autobiography, make sure it's free of the mistakes that can spoil otherwise good writing. Use this checklist to help you.

Conventions

☐ Make sure the names of specific people and places are capitalized.

☐ Make sure sentences end with correct punctuation.

☐ Check sentence structure and fix fragments.

Publishing

Use this checklist to prepare to present your autobiography.

Presentation

☐ Have one other person read your autobiography. Consider their suggestions and make changes if needed.

☐ Think about adding graphics, drawings, or pictures to make your autobiography more interesting.

☐ Neatly rewrite or, if you are using a computer, print the final copy of your autobiography.

☐ Share your autobiography with your audience.

☐ Other __**Answers may describe any other way students will be sharing or publishing their autobiographies.**__

THE WRITING PROCESS

UNIT 2 Astronomy • **Lesson I** *Galileo*

Writing a Summary

Objective: Students prewrite for a summary.

Use the writing process to write an expository summary.

Prewriting

Who is the audience for your summary?

☐ Your teacher

☐ Your classmates

☐ A friend

☐ Other _____ **Audience should be specific. Students' answers may include themselves, an audience assigned by you, another class, a family member, or readers of a school newspaper.**

What is your purpose for writing?

☐ To use it as a study tool to help remember important information

☐ To share interesting information with someone

☐ To help analyze a piece of writing

☐ Other _____ **Purpose should be clearly stated. Students' answers may include *to learn about a subject, to help under-stand the subject better, to help in writing a book review*, or *to help in writing a report***

Plan your summary on the next page. List the main idea of the original work at the top of the graphic organizer. The main idea should be in your own words. Write the key details that support the main idea in the boxes.

UNIT 2 Astronomy • **Lesson 1** *Galileo*

Objective: Students complete a graphic organizer and draft their expository summaries.

EXPOSITORY WRITING

▶ **Writing a Summary**

Main Idea _____

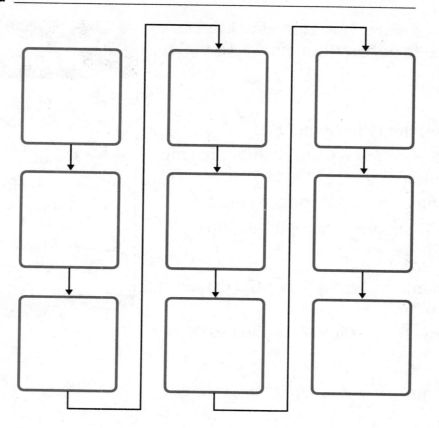

Drafting

Use your graphic organizer to write your summary. Write a sentence about each main point shown in your graphic organizer. Use only essential facts and details. Add a concluding sentence to tie together all the main points.

The main idea should be short and to the point. Details should support the main idea.

UNIT 2 Astronomy • **Lesson I** *Galileo*

Objective: Students revise their summaries.

Revising

Reread your summary. Use this checklist to improve it. Use proofreading marks to make the changes.

Ideas

☐ Does your summary have one main idea?

☐ Is your summary to the point, without having extra information?

☐ Did you include all the important details?

☐ Do the details support the topic sentence?

Organization

☐ Does your summary group essential details in a logical order?

☐ Do your ideas flow from one to the next?

Voice

☐ Does the summary sound like *you* wrote it?

Word Choice

☐ Did you use your own words? Are any words or phrases too similar to those of the original?

☐ Do your words show the meaning that was intended in the original work?

Sentence Fluency

☐ Do your sentences flow from one to the next, or do they sound choppy?

☐ Can you combine any sentences for a better flow?

☐ Other **May include questions related to a summary.**

	Proofreading Marks
¶	Indent.
∧	Add something.
ℓ	Take something out.
∽	Transpose.
≡	Make a capital letter.
sp	Check spelling.
⊙	Add a period.

Make all your changes to your summary. Add anything else you think your summary needs. If you have made many revisions, rewrite your summary.

Objective: Students edit and publish their summaries.

▶ **Writing a Summary**

Editing/Proofreading

Proofread your summary. Careless mistakes can confuse your readers so that they do not understand the main idea. Use this checklist to help you.

Conventions

☐ Did you check the spelling of any proper names or specialized words against the original piece of writing?

☐ Does each sentence have the correct punctuation?

☐ Is each sentence complete?

☐ Other **May include questions about grammar, usage, and mechanics specific to expository writing.**

Publishing

Use this checklist to get your summary ready for publishing.

Presentation

☐ Reread your summary to make sure it is complete.

☐ Copy your summary onto a clean sheet of paper, or type it on a computer.

☐ Do a final check for spelling and mechanics errors.

☐ Make sure your summary is neat and easy to read.

☐ Write reference information about the original source, **Tell students** if necessary. **whether you want them to include this.**

☐ Other **May include questions about required guidelines.**

☐ Present your summary to your audience.
Tell students to whom they should present their summaries, based upon the audience that they chose or that you assigned. You may want to have students submit their summaries to the school newspaper or have them read their summaries for the class.

EXPOSITORY WRITING

Objective: Students plan to write a response to nonfiction.

Writing a Response to Nonfiction

Write an essay responding to nonfiction.

Prewriting

Who is the audience for your response to nonfiction essay?

☐ Your teacher

☐ Your classmates

☐ A friend

☐ Other ___Audience should be specific. Students' answers may include themselves, an audience assigned by you, a pen pal, a family member, or the school.

What is your purpose for writing?

☐ To tell someone what you thought of a piece of writing

☐ To question something you read

☐ To show how you would respond in the situation you read about

☐ To show a strong reaction to something you read

☐ Other ___Purpose should be clearly stated. Students may choose to respond to only part of the nonfiction selection, perhaps a part that is meaningful to them. Keep in mind that responses can come in a variety of forms—whatever the student gets out of the work.

Use the graphic organizer on the next page to help you write down the main idea and details of the nonfiction selection. You will use this organizer to help you respond to the selection.

UNIT 2 Astronomy • **Lesson 2** *Telescopes*

▶ **Writing a Response to Nonfiction**

Objective: Students organize their ideas for a response to a nonfiction work.

EXPOSITORY WRITING

Topic

Subtopic

1. _____
2. _____
3. _____

Subtopic

1. _____
2. _____
3. _____

Subtopic

1. _____
2. _____
3. _____

Subtopic

1. _____
2. _____
3. _____

Conclusion

Drafting

Write your response on a sheet of paper. Use the
subtopics and details from your graphic organizer to
guide you through your response.

Name _____ Date _____

Writing a Response to Nonfiction

Revising

Reread your summary. Use the checklist below to help you improve your response. Use proofreading marks to make changes.

Proofreading Marks

¶	Indent
∧	Add something.
ℰ	Take something out.
∼	Transpose.
≡	Make a capital letter.
sp	Check spelling.
⊙	Add a period.

Ideas

☐ Is your main idea or angle of your response clear and focused?

☐ Did you support your ideas with examples and details?

☐ Are you responding only to the original work?

Organization

☐ Will the reader be able to follow your ideas from one to the next?

☐ Do all of your details support your main idea?

Voice

☐ Do your words show that you feel a certain way about the nonfiction selection (for example, excited or interested)?

Word Choice

☐ Did you use your own words?

☐ Did you use words that describe exactly what you mean, or can you add more details?

Sentence Fluency

☐ Have you used transitional phrases to link your sentences?

☐ Can you combine any sentences for a better flow?

☐ Other **Should include questions related to the type of response that the student has written.**

Mark all of your changes on your paper. Add anything else you think your response needs. Rewrite it if you made many changes.

UNIT 2 Astronomy • **Lesson 2** *Telescopes*

> **Writing a Response to Nonfiction**

Editing/Proofreading

Proofread your response to nonfiction. Use the checklist below to help you.

Conventions

☐ Did you capitalize the proper nouns, including titles of literary works and events?

☐ Does each sentence have the correct punctuation?

☐ Did you use complete sentences?

☐ Did you check for spelling errors, including those missed by a spell checker?

☐ Other **May include questions about grammar, usage, and mechanics specific to students' work.**

Publishing

Use this checklist to get your response ready for publishing.

Presentation

☐ Rewrite your response on a clean sheet of paper or use a computer to type your work.

☐ Do a final check for spelling and punctuation errors.

☐ Add diagrams or pictures to help explain anything, if necessary.

☐ Present your response to nonfiction by using one of the following methods:
  • Publish your response on the school Web site.
  • Read your response to the class.
  • Place your response in a class book.
  • Keep your response in your Writing Folder.

You may wish to give students another method for presenting their work.

☐ Other **May include items about required guidelines. May include other ways of presenting work.**

Objective: Students edit and publish their responses to nonfiction.

EXPOSITORY WRITING

Objective: Students plan for a book review.

UNIT 2 Astronomy • **Lesson 3** *The Heavenly Zoo*

Writing a Book Review

Use the writing process to write a book review.

Prewriting

Who is the audience for your book review?

☐ Your teacher

☐ Your classmates

☐ A friend

☐ Readers of the school newspaper

☐ Other _____ **Audience should be specific. Students' answers may include an audience assigned by you or a family member.**

What is your purpose for writing?

☐ To share a book you liked

☐ To tell about a book you did not like

☐ To encourage others to read the book

☐ To understand a character in the book

☐ To analyze the book so that you understand it better

☐ Other **Purpose should be clearly stated.** _____

Fill in the information about the story you are reviewing.

Author's Name _____
Title of Book or Story _____
Date of Publication _____
Main Subject of Book or Story _____
_____

UNIT 2 Astronomy • **Lesson 3** *The Heavenly Zoo*

Objective: Students prewrite for a book review.

▶ **Writing a Book Review**

Make sure you understand the content of the book you are reviewing. Then, complete the organizer below to tell what you know and give your opinions.

EXPOSITORY WRITING

Author's Purpose ▶ Students should state the author's goal in writing. This might be the theme (for a story) or main idea (for a nonfiction work).

Summary: Key Points ▶ Students should give a brief synopsis of the plot or narrative. You may want to have them complete a concept map in order to do this.

Highlight a Feature ▶ Students should give an example of an inviting feature. *"The most amazing part . . ."*

Opinions
Did the author achieve his or her purpose? Give examples. What were your favorite parts? Did the theme appeal to you? Were the word choice and tone appropriate for the audience?
▶

Encourage students to write other opinions. Make sure students give reasons for their opinions.

Recommendations
Did you like or dislike? Why? Do you recommend this? Why?
▶ Students should comment on features that make the book appealing or unappealing and recommend the book based on the opinions above.

Drafting

Write your book review on a sheet of paper.

► **Writing a Book Review**

Objective: Students revise their book reviews.

Revising

Reread your book review. Look for ways to make your review better. Use this checklist to help you. Use proofreading marks to make the changes.

Ideas

☐ Does your opening give your subject?

☐ Does your opening make the reader want to read on?

☐ Are your opinions explained with examples?

☐ Do you think your ideas will convince the reader to read (or not read) the book or story?

☐ Did you tell so much of the original that it might ruin the enjoyment for your readers?

Organization

☐ Are your ideas arranged in a logical order?

☐ Do all ideas related to each topic go together?

Voice

☐ Can your readers tell your feelings about the book (for example, enthusiasm or disappointment)?

☐ Do you sound confident about your opinions?

Word Choice and Sentence Fluency

☐ Did you use descriptive words to help the reader understand exactly what you mean?

☐ Are your sentences smooth and easy to read?

☐ Did you combine sentences for a better flow?

☐ Other **May include questions relating to including nonessential information or expanding parts.**

Mark all changes on your paper. Add anything else you think your review needs. Write a new copy if you have made many changes.

Proofreading Marks	
¶	Indent
∧	Add something.
ℓ	Take something out.
∼	Transpose.
≡	Make a capital letter.
sp	Check spelling.
⊙	Add a period.

UNIT 2 Astronomy • **Lesson 3** *The Heavenly Zoo*

▶ **Writing a Book Review**

Editing/Proofreading

Proofread your book review. Use this checklist to help you.

Conventions

☐ Did you spell the title and author's name correctly?

☐ Does each sentence have the correct punctuation?

☐ Did you check for spelling errors, including those missed by a spell checker?

☐ Other **May include questions about grammar, usage, and mechanics specific to students' work.**

Publishing

Use this checklist to get your book review ready for publishing.

Presentation

☐ Copy your book review onto a clean sheet of paper or type it on a computer. Make sure it is neat and easy to read. If you have different sections in your review, add headings that will stand out. Add anything else to make the format pleasing to the eye.

☐ If you wish, provide illustrations for your review. You may want to include a photo of the cover or of the author.

☐ Reread your book review a final time for mistakes.

☐ Present your response by using one of the following methods:
  • Check your public library to see if you can post it there.
  • Put the review together in a book with other students' reviews. Keep it in the classroom or give it to your school library.
  • Read your review to the class. Have a copy of the book to pass around during your presentation.
  • E-mail or send your review to a friend.

☐ Other **You may want to provide alternative publishing options.**

EXPOSITORY WRITING

Objective: Students prewrite for an expository essay.

Writing an Expository Essay

Use the writing process to write an expository essay.

Prewriting

Who is the audience for your essay?

☐ Your teacher

☐ Your classmates

☐ A student organization

☐ Readers of the school newspaper

☐ The judges of an essay contest

☐ Other __Audience should be specific.__

What is your purpose for writing?

☐ To learn more about a topic

☐ To explain something to a person who does not know about it

☐ Other __Purpose should be clearly stated.__

Conduct research and take notes for your essay. Use the chart below to keep a record of the sources you used.

Title	Author	Year	Place	Publisher	Pages
Allow students time to conduct research. They should take notes on several points to support the main topic. You may want to explain how to find the publication year, place, and publisher for a work.					

Objective: Students complete a graphic organizer for an expository essay.

► **Writing an Expository Essay**

Use the graphic organizer to help organize your thoughts and research. Write the topic of your essay and fill in the subtopics that support the main topic. Include details from your research under each subtopic.

Topic

Subtopic   **Subtopic**

Students should organize their notes into this graphic organizer. They should have several subtopics and details about each subtopic. They should include only pertinent topics and details. After organizing their ideas, students should think of a conclusion based on their key points. You may wish to have students write a bibliography using their sources from page 18.

1. _____   1. _____
2. _____   2. _____
3. _____   3. _____

Subtopic   **Subtopic**

1. _____   1. _____
2. _____   2. _____
3. _____   3. _____

Conclusion

Drafting

Write your essay on a sheet of paper. Use the facts and details from your graphic organizer to help you.

EXPOSITORY WRITING

Objective: Students revise their expository essays.

Revising

▶ **Writing an Expository Essay**

Reread your essay. Use this checklist to help you improve it. Use proofreading marks to make changes.

Ideas

☐ Will your audience understand what your purpose or main focus is?

☐ Do all of the subtopics support your main focus?

☐ Are all of your details related to each subtopic?

☐ Did you include your thoughts and opinions?

☐ Does your conclusion summarize your ideas?

Organization

☐ Is there a clear structure to the essay—opening, subtopics and details, and conclusion?

☐ Are your subtopics in a logical order? If your ideas jump around, reorder them.

Voice

☐ Does your personality come through in your writing?

Word Choice

☐ Did you use exact words to give your audience a clear idea of your topics and details?

☐ Did you define words your audience might not know?

Sentence Fluency

☐ Did you use transition words to show when you move from one topic or detail to the next?

☐ Other **May include questions relating to amount of research. Students may need to conduct more research on their topics after revising.**

Mark changes to your essay. Add anything else you think it needs.

Proofreading Marks	
⌐P	Indent
∧	Add something.
ℓ	Take something out.
~	Transpose.
≡	Make a capital letter.
sp	Check spelling.
⊙	Add a period.

Objective: Students edit and publish their expository essays.

Editing/Proofreading

▶ **Writing an Expository Essay**

Proofread your essay. Use this checklist to help you.

Conventions

☐ Did you capitalize proper nouns?

☐ Does each sentence have the correct punctuation, including commas in places and dates?

☐ Did you check for spelling errors, including those missed by a spell checker?

☐ Have you checked the spellings of special names against the original source?

☐ Other __**May include questions about grammar, usage, and mechanics specific to the essay.**__

Publishing

Use this checklist to get your essay ready for publishing.

Presentation

☐ Rewrite your essay on a clean sheet of paper, or use a computer to type it.

☐ Reread your essay. Do a final check for spelling and punctuation errors. Make sure you feel it is complete.

☐ Check to make sure the finished product is visually appealing.
  • Is it easy to read?
  • Do you need to add illustrations to make your essay more interesting?
  • Do you want to add a title page or cover?

☐ Present your essay by using one of the following methods:
  • Read your essay to your audience.
  • Place your essay in your Writing Folder.
  • Submit your essay to the school newspaper or to a contest.

☐ Other __**May include guidelines you gave.**__

EXPOSITORY WRITING

Objective: Students begin to plan for a research report.

Writing a Research Report

Use the writing process to write a research report.

Prewriting

Who is the audience for your report?

☐ An organization you want to inform

☐ Your teacher

☐ Your classmates

☐ Magazine readers

☐ Other __**Audience should be specific. If students made a selection from above, encourage them to write the specific audience here, for example, *Humane Society* or *Time Magazine for Kids*.**__

What is your purpose for writing?

☐ To learn more about a subject

☐ To explain to others about a subject

☐ Other __**Purpose should be clearly stated. Encourage students to include information on a specific topic, for example, *to explain about new research on genes*.**__

What is your topic?

Write questions that you would like your report to answer.

1. _____

2. **Students should use a variety of sources, such as magazine articles, books, and the Internet. Be sure**

3. ~~**they know to use the most current information**~~ **they**

4. **can find.**

Decide what sources you will use to find the answers. Keep track of them on a separate sheet of paper.

Take notes from your sources using note cards. Note only the information important to your report's main idea.

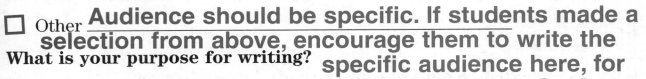

Objective: Students prewrite for a research report.

EXPOSITORY WRITING

▶ Writing a Research Report

Use your notes to plan your research report.

Topic

[ ]

Subtopic

[ ]

Subtopic

[ ]

Allow students time to conduct research. They should organize their notes into the graphic organizer by including subtopics and details. Students should come up with the idea for the conclusion before they draft.

1. _____
2. _____
3. _____

1. _____
2. _____
3. _____

Subtopic

[ ]

Subtopic

[ ]

1. _____
2. _____
3. _____

1. _____
2. _____
3. _____

Conclusion

[ ]

Drafting

Write a draft of your research report. Your introduction should identify the focus. Each paragraph should support the main idea. Each subtopic can serve as the topic sentence of a paragraph. End your report with a summary of the main points and a strong closing sentence.

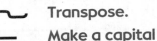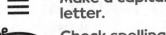

Writing a Research Report

Objective: Students revise their research reports.

Revising

Reread your report. Mark any changes to improve it. Use this checklist to help.

Ideas

☐ Does your introduction state the main idea or focus of your report?

☐ Does all the information support your focus?

☐ Does your research answer all the basic questions about your topic?

☐ Did you use examples and quotations to support important points in your report?

☐ Do you need to clarify any information by adding charts or diagrams?

☐ Does your conclusion summarize your main points?

Organization

☐ Are your subtopics arranged in a logical order?

☐ Does each paragraph have a topic sentence and supporting details?

Voice

☐ Do you sound confident about your knowledge?

Word Choice

☐ Do you use transition words to tie together ideas?

☐ Have you left out words such as *I think*? Your report should include only the facts you found in your sources.

Sentence Fluency

☐ Are your sentences smooth and easy to read?

☐ Other **May include questions relating to clarifying, adding, or deleting text.**

Mark your changes on your report.

Proofreading Marks

¶	Indent
∧	Add something.
ℓ	Take something out.
∼	Transpose.
≡	Make a capital letter.
⌢sp	Check spelling.
⊙	Add a period.

Editing/Proofreading   ▶ **Writing a Research Report**

EXPOSITORY WRITING

Objective: Students edit and publish their research reports.

Proofread your research report. Use this checklist to help you.

Conventions

☐ Double-check all the facts you used.

☐ Check for spelling errors, including those missed by a spell checker.

☐ Check that any specialized words are spelled correctly.

☐ Did you punctuate correctly, including parentheses, hyphens, dashes, and ellipses?

☐ Other **May include questions specific to students' work or what they are studying in grammar, usage, and mechanics.**

Publishing

Use this checklist to get your research report ready for publishing.

Presentation

☐ Rewrite or type your report on a computer so that it looks neat and is easy to read.

☐ Format your report so that it is easy to read.
  • Number your pages, starting with the first page of text.
  • Double-space the entire paper and leave the correct margin. **Give students tips on formatting.**

☐ Reread your report for spelling and punctuation errors.

☐ Add any diagrams or illustrations to make your ideas clearer or to add interest to your report.

☐ Prepare a title page and bibliography if they are required.

☐ Present your report by using one of the following methods:
  • Read your report to the class. **May include**
  • Submit your report to a magazine. **required guidelines**

☐ Other **or additional ways to present the report.**

Writing an Analysis of Fiction

Objective: Students plan to write an analysis of fiction.

Use the writing process to write an analysis of fiction.

Prewriting

Who is the audience for your analysis?

☐ Your teacher

☐ Your classmates

☐ A friend

☐ Other _____ Audience should be specific. Students' answers may include themselves, an audience assigned by you, a pen pal, a family member, or the school.

What is your purpose for writing?

☐ To explain the plot to someone

☐ To understand the plot better

☐ To analyze the plot

☐ Other _____ Purpose should be clearly stated. Students may choose to analyze a character instead.

Objective: Students prewrite an analysis of fiction.

► **Writing an Analysis of Fiction**

Analyze the plot using the graphic organizer below. Fill in the characters, setting, problem, climax, and resolution.

Plot Line

_____
_____

If students chose to analyze a character, have them complete a web instead. A web can be found on Language Arts Transparency 10.

Climax

_____
_____
_____
_____
_____

**Characters
Setting
Problem**

Resolution

_____
_____

Drafting

Use the graphic organizer to help you write your analysis of fiction.

- Start by explaining the characters, setting, and problem.
- Continue by describing the problem, or conflict.
- Then, tell about the climax and give the resolution.
- Finally, add concluding remarks to leave the reader with something to think about.

EXPOSITORY WRITING

Name _____ Date _____

UNIT 2   Astronomy • **Lesson 7** *The Book That Saved the Earth*

▶ 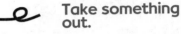 **Writing an Analysis of Fiction**

Revising

Reread your analysis. Use this checklist to help you improve it. Use proofreading marks to make the changes.

Ideas

☐ Does your opening tell what you are analyzing?

☐ Do you tell the problem in the beginning of your response?

☐ Have you included all the important details related to the problem, and resolution?

☐ Is the conflict that you describe the *main* problem?

☐ Have you included too many details?

Proofreading Marks	
¶	Indent
∧	Add something.
ℰ	Take something out.
∿	Transpose.
═	Make a capital letter.
sp ◯	Check spelling.
⊙	Add a period.

Organization

☐ Do you describe the plot in the same order as the events happened in the story?

☐ Does each paragraph have a main idea?

Voice

☐ Does your writing make the reader care about your topic?

Word Choice

☐ Did you use your own words?

Sentence Fluency

☐ Can you combine sentences or add words to make your sentences less choppy?

☐ Other __May include questions relating to clarity of__ details or presenting the problem and resolution clearly, without extra ideas.

Mark your changes on your analysis. If you made many changes, rewrite it.

28   UNIT 2 • Lesson 7   *Writing an Analysis of Fiction* • **Writer's Workbook**

Objective: Students revise their analyses of fiction.

Objective: Students edit and publish their analyses of fiction.

► **Writing an Analysis of Fiction**

Editing/Proofreading

Proofread your analysis. Use this checklist to help you.

Conventions

☐ Have you spelled the character and place names correctly?

☐ Did you check for other spelling errors?

☐ Does each sentence have the correct end punctuation?

☐ Did you use commas correctly?

☐ Other **May include questions about grammar, usage, and mechanics specific to what students are writing.**

Publishing

Use this checklist to get your analysis ready for publishing.

Presentation

☐ Copy your work onto a clean sheet of paper, or type it on a computer.

☐ Reread your paper for spelling and punctuation errors.

☐ Check to make sure it is neat and the format is easy to read.

☐ Present your response by using one of the following methods:
  • Place it in your Writing Folder.
  • Share it with a classmate.
  • Present it to your teacher.
  • Save it to help you study for a test.

☐ Other **May include questions about required guidelines.**

EXPOSITORY WRITING

UNIT 3 Heritage • **Lesson 1** *The Land I Lost*

Writing a Description

Use the writing process to write a descriptive paragraph.

Prewriting

Who is the audience for your description?

☐ Your teacher

☐ A friend

☐ Yourself

☐ Readers of the school newspaper

☐ Other **Audience should be specific.** _____

What is your purpose for writing?

☐ To tell about a place you love

☐ To write a tribute about a person

☐ To make your reader visualize a person, place, or thing

☐ To tell about an event to someone who did not experience it

☐ To write about a place for a travel brochure

☐ To remember a particular person, place, or thing

☐ Other **Purpose should be clearly stated. There are many reasons why a student could write a descriptive paragraph.**

What order will you use to present your details?

☐ Near to far

☐ Far to near

☐ Top to bottom

☐ First thing that happened to last thing that happened

☐ Most noticeable thing first

☐ Most important to least important

☐ Other **Accept any logical order.** _____

UNIT 3 Heritage • **Lesson I** *The Land I Lost*

▶ **Writing a Description**

Fill in your subject in the first box of the graphic organizer below. Then complete the graphic organizer with the details that you will describe. Be sure to put the details in the order that you chose on page 30.

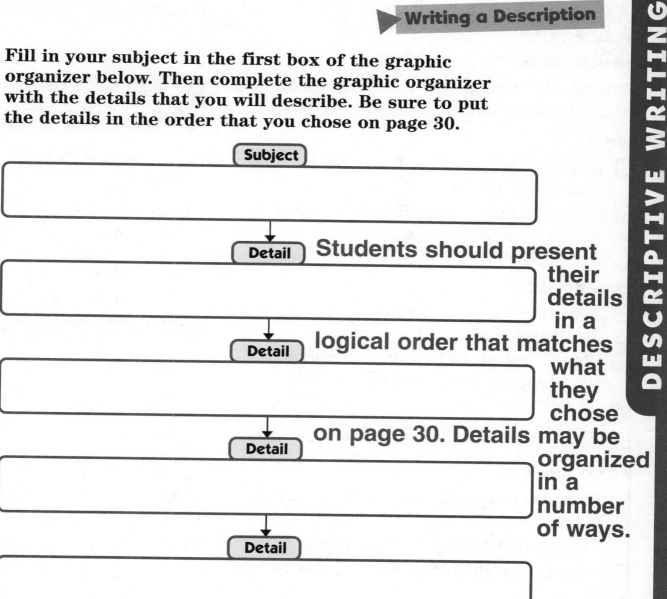

Subject

Detail Students should present their details in a logical order that matches what they chose on page 30. Details may be organized in a number of ways.

Detail

Detail

Detail

Drafting

Use the graphic organizer above to write your description on loose-leaf paper.
- Write a topic sentence so that your reader knows what you are describing.
- Turn each of your details into sentences. Make sure you keep your details in order.
- Develop each detail by appealing to the senses.

Objective: Students complete a graphic organizer and a draft for a descriptive paragraph.

DESCRIPTIVE WRITING

▶ Writing a Description

Objective: Students revise their descriptive paragraphs.

Revising

Reread your paragraph. Use this checklist to help you improve your descriptive writing.

Ideas

☐ Will your audience be able to tell what you are describing?

☐ Do you provide enough details so that your reader can get a picture of what you are describing?

Organization

☐ Does your description group details in a way that makes sense?

☐ Did you use words to make the sentences work together, such as location words?

Voice

☐ Does your description sound like *you* wrote it?

Word Choice

☐ Have you chosen descriptive words that have sensory appeal?

☐ Can you make your adjectives, nouns, or verbs more exact?

☐ Can you add similes or metaphors to describe *how?*

Sentence Fluency

☐ Can you add any transitions from one sentence to the next?

☐ Other **May include questions related to the specific topic, either a person, place, thing, or event.**

Mark your changes to your paragraph. Rewrite your paragraph if you've made many changes.

Proofreading Marks	
∧	Add something.
ℯ	Take something out.
⁓	Transpose.
☰	Make a capital letter.
⌀	Check spelling.
⊙	Add a period.

UNIT 3 Heritage • **Lesson I** *The Land I Lost*

▶ **Writing a Description**

Objective: Students edit and publish their descriptive paragraphs.

Editing/Proofreading

Proofread your description. Use this checklist to help you.

Conventions

☐ Does your paragraph have any spelling errors?

☐ Did you capitalize all proper nouns?

☐ Does each sentence have the correct end punctuation?

☐ Did you use commas correctly between descriptive words?

☐ Other **May include questions about grammar, usage, and mechanics specific to what students are studying.**

Publishing

Use this checklist to get your description ready for publishing.

Presentation

☐ Rewrite your description onto a clean sheet of paper, or type it on a computer.

☐ Read your description for any final errors.

☐ If you wish, use drawings, photos, or computer graphics to illustrate the description.

☐ Present your description by using one of the following methods.
  • Give the description to your audience.
  • Place it in your writing portfolio.
  • Read your description to your classmates. Have them draw the subject of your description after you read it. Check to see whether their pictures show what you thought you described.

☐ Other **May include other ways to present the description. For example, if students are writing about people they admire, you could make a class book or display the descriptions at a family open house.**

Name _____ Date _____

Writing an Observation Report

Use the writing process to write an observation report about a scene. Gather information by using your five senses.

Prewriting

Who is the audience for your observation report?

☐ Your teacher

☐ Your parent

☐ A friend

☐ Yourself

☐ Readers of the school newspaper

☐ Judges in a contest

☐ Other __Audience should be specific._____

What is your purpose for writing?

☐ To explain why something happens

☐ To give the results of an experiment

☐ To describe an event

☐ To describe a scene

☐ To record something memorable in your journal

☐ Other __Purpose should be clearly stated._____

What is the topic of your observation report?
Students' responses should be specific, for example, watching eggs hatch. If students are conducting an experiment, the topic should be their hypothesis.

▶ **Writing an Observation Report**

DESCRIPTIVE WRITING

Objective: Students prewrite and draft for an observation report.

Complete the graphic organizer below to organize your observation. List all of the sensory details that describe your subject. Write your events or details in the order in which they happened.

	Sights	Sounds	Smells	Tastes	Textures
1	Students will actually need to observe something for this assignment. Allow students extra time to observe a scene or event or to set up an experiment. All of the senses might not be represented in one report.				
2					
3					
4					
5					

Drafting

Write your observation report on a sheet of paper. Turn your ideas into sentences by sharing all of the details for either one row or one column in the table above. Then write all the details in the next row or column. This way, your report will move naturally from either one sense to another or from one observation to another. Show, don't tell, what the scene is like—what it feels, smells, tastes, and sounds like, as well as what it looks like.

Name _____ Date _____

▶ **Writing an Observation Report**

Revising

Reread your observation report. Look for ways that your report might be made clearer to your audience. Use this checklist.

Ideas

☐ Is your topic stated in the beginning?

☐ If you reported on an experiment, did you include your hypothesis at the beginning?

☐ Did you state all of the important observations?

☐ Can you add any charts or graphs to display your facts?

Organization

☐ Did you arrange your supporting details in order as they happened or in another logical order?

Voice

☐ Is your voice too informal? Will your audience take you seriously?

Word Choice

☐ Did you use precise words to describe the details? Do your adjectives and adverbs tell exactly what you observed?

☐ Did you use place and location words to help the reader see what you are observing?

Sentence Fluency

☐ Are your sentences smooth and easy to read? If not, add transition words to link separate ideas.

☐ Other **May include questions related to the particular topic or event.**

Mark the changes on your report. Rewrite your report if you made many changes.

Proofreading Marks	
¶	Indent.
∧	Add something.
℮	Take something out.
∼	Transpose.
≡	Make a capital letter.
sp	Check spelling.
⊙	Add a period.

UNIT 3 Heritage • **Lesson 2** *In Two Worlds/History of the Tunrit*

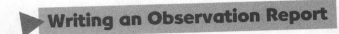

Editing/Proofreading

Proofread your observation report. Use this checklist to help you.

Conventions

☐ Have you corrected spelling errors?

☐ Did you use correct paragraph indentation?

☐ Did you use commas and end punctuation marks correctly?

☐ Did you use adjectives and adverbs correctly?

☐ Other **May include questions related to students' writing.**

Publishing

Use this checklist to get your report ready for publishing.

Presentation

☐ Copy your observation report onto a clean sheet of paper, or type it on a computer.

☐ Add any charts or graphs that will show your data.

☐ Reread your report a final time for errors.

☐ Present your report by using one of the following methods:
- Submit it to a science or writing magazine.
- Send it to a Web publishing program for young people.
- Present it to your class.
- Submit it as part of a science fair project.

☐ Other **May include questions about required guidelines or other forms of presentation.**

DESCRIPTIVE WRITING

UNIT 3 Heritage • **Lesson 3** *The West Side*

Writing a Lyric Poem

Use the writing process to write a lyric poem.

Prewriting

Who is the audience for your poem?

☐ Your teacher

☐ A family member

☐ Yourself

☐ A friend

☐ Your classmates

☐ Readers of a poetry magazine

☐ Readers of the school newspaper

☐ Other __**Audience should be specific.**__

What is your purpose for writing?

☐ To tell your feelings about something

☐ To write a song

☐ To describe something special

☐ To show strong feelings about something

☐ To share an experience with other people

☐ Other __**Purpose should be clearly stated.**__

What will the topic of your lyric poem be?

_____

Objective: Students prewrite for a lyric poem.

UNIT 3 Heritage • **Lesson 3** *The West Side*

▶ **Writing a Lyric Poem**

P O E T R Y

Think of ways to describe your subject. List them as details in the cluster below. Use the senses to think of the details.

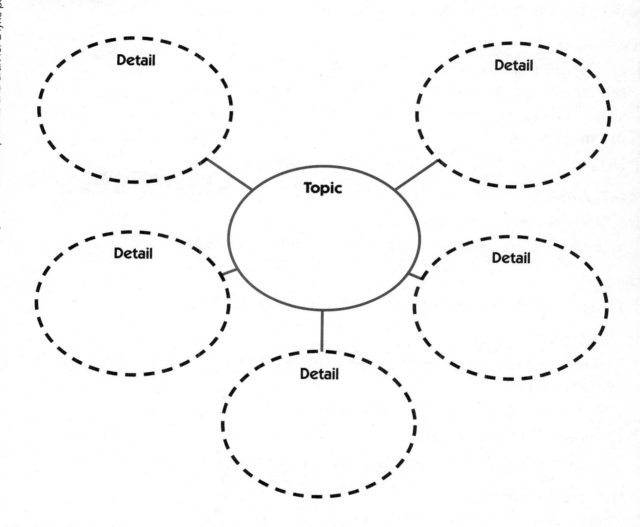

Drafting

Write your lyric poem on a sheet of paper. Put your details above into a poetic format. Create line breaks where you naturally hear pauses when reading. Write a final line that will leave the reader with a feeling or make an effect on the reader that reflects your main focus.

UNIT 3 Heritage • **Lesson 3** *The West Side*

▶ **Writing a Lyric Poem**

Objective: Students revise their lyric poem.

Revising

Reread your poem. Add or change the poem so that it shares your thoughts the way you want it to. Use the following checklist.

Ideas

☐ Does your poem say what you mean? Will the reader be able to understand what you mean?

☐ Will your poem give your audience a feeling of completeness?

☐ Do you use sensory details to create images?

Organization

☐ Is there a pattern to your lines?

☐ Would your images make better sense in another order?

Voice

☐ Does the poem show your true feelings about your topic?

Word Choice

☐ Did you use sensory words to bring images to your reader's mind?

☐ Do your words have an effective sound?

☐ Do your lines have rhythm?

☐ Do you use similes or metaphors to explain an idea?

Sentence Fluency

☐ Do the lines sound like they belong together?

☐ Other **May include questions relating to adding ideas, rewording for better effect, the form of the poem, and the effectiveness of the title.**

Mark your changes on your poem. You may want to rewrite your poem if you have made many changes.

Proofreading Marks	
∧	Add something.
ℓ	Take something out.
∽	Transpose.
✀	Check spelling.
⊙	Add a period.

▶ **Writing a Lyric Poem**

Editing/Proofreading

Proofread your poem. Use this checklist to help you.

Conventions

☐ Does your poem have any spelling errors?

☐ Did you begin each line with a capital letter?

☐ Did you use commas and end punctuation correctly?

☐ Did you use prepositions correctly?

☐ Other **May include questions about grammar or usage, including subject-verb agreement and structure of lines in poetry.**

Publishing

Use this checklist to get your poem ready for publishing.

Presentation

☐ Copy your poem onto a clean sheet of paper. You may want to use a special note card or decorated paper.

☐ Check for spelling and mechanics errors.

☐ Add any illustrations or decorations that you wish.

☐ Present your poem by using one of the following methods:
  • Place it in a collection of class poetry.
  • Place it in your writing portfolio.
  • Give it to the person for whom you wrote it.
  • Mail it to a magazine for a contest. **A number of magazines hold contests or print young people's original stories and poems.**
  • Share your poem by performing it. Read it to your class or another class.
  • Set it to music and sing it for your audience.
  • Post your work on a poetry Web site for young people.
  • Keep it in your personal journal.

☐ Other **May include additional ways to present a poem.**

POETRY

Name _____ Date _____

Objective: Students plan for the writing of a quatrain.

Writing a Quatrain

Use the writing process to write a quatrain.

Prewriting

Who is the audience for your quatrain?

☐ Your teacher

☐ A family member

☐ Yourself

☐ A friend

☐ Your classmates

☐ Readers of a poetry magazine

☐ Readers of the school newspaper

☐ Other **Audience should be specific.** _____

What is your purpose for writing a quatrain?

☐ To express a thought in rhyme

☐ To entertain by writing a verse for a greeting card

☐ To explain an idea

☐ To add to your journal or portfolio

☐ Other **Purpose should be clearly stated.** _____

What is the topic of your quatrain?

_____

UNIT 3 Heritage • **Lesson 4** *Love as Strong as Ginger/Women*

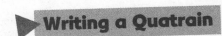

Write details about your topic on the lines below.

_____

_____

_____

_____

_____

_____

Drafting

Write your quatrain on a sheet of paper using your ideas from above. Choose a rhyme pattern for your four lines.

Objective: Students prewrite and draft for a quatrain.

POETRY

Objective: Students revise their quatrain.

▶ **Writing a Quatrain**

Revising

Reread your quatrain. Use the following checklist to help you revise it.

Ideas

☐ Does your quatrain express just one thought or idea?

☐ Did you convey the feelings you wanted to about that one idea?

Organization

☐ Do the lines have a particular rhyming pattern?

☐ Does the order of your lines make sense?

Voice

☐ Does your quatrain sound like *you* wrote it?

☐ Does it sound like you really have something to say about the topic?

Word Choice

☐ Are your words precise and descriptive?

☐ Did you use any other sounds of language, such as alliteration, assonance, or repetition?

Sentence Fluency

☐ Do the lines sound like they belong together?

☐ Do your lines have rhythm?

☐ Other **May include questions related to adding ideas, rewording for better effect, and rhyme.**

Make your corrections on your paper. Rewrite your quatrain if you have made many changes.

Proofreading Marks

∧	Add something.
℮	Take something out.
∼	Transpose.
sp ⊙	Check spelling.
⊙	Add a period.

► **Writing a Quatrain**

Editing/Proofreading

Proofread your quatrain. Use this checklist to help you.

Conventions

☐ Does your quatrain have any spelling errors?

☐ Does it have four lines?

☐ Other **May include questions about grammar, usage, and mechanics specific to writing poetry.**

Publishing

Use this checklist to get your quatrain ready for publishing.

Presentation

☐ Reread your quatrain to make sure you feel good about it from start to finish.

☐ Copy your poem onto a clean sheet of paper. You may want to use a special note card or decorated paper.

☐ Check for spelling and mechanics errors.

☐ Add any illustrations or decorations that you wish.

☐ Present your poem by using one of the following methods:
  • Place it in a collection of class poetry.
  • Place it in your writing portfolio.
  • Give it to the person for whom you wrote it.
  • Mail it to a magazine for a contest. **A number of magazines hold contests or print young people's original stories and poems.**
  • Share your poem by performing it. Read it to your class or another class.
  • Post your work on a poetry Web site for young people.
  • Keep it in your personal journal.

☐ Other **May include additional ways to present a poem.**

Objective: Students edit and publish their quatrain.

POETRY

UNIT 3 Heritage • **Lesson 5** *The Night Journey*

Writing a Free-Verse Poem

Objective: Students plan for the writing of a free-verse poem.

Use the writing process to write a free-verse poem.

Prewriting

Who is the audience for your free-verse poem?

☐ Your teacher

☐ A family member

☐ A friend

☐ Your classmates

☐ Readers of a poetry magazine

☐ Club members

☐ Other **Audience should be specific.** _____

What is your purpose for writing your free-verse poem?

☐ To express ideas and images

☐ To make someone happy

☐ To explain a thought

☐ To remember a certain feeling (for example, happiness or sadness)

☐ Other **Purpose should be clearly stated.** _____

UNIT 3 Heritage • **Lesson 5** *The Night Journey*

▶ **Writing a Free-Verse Poem**

POETRY

Objective: Students complete a graphic organizer and a draft for a poem.

Complete the cluster below to plan for your poem.
Write your topic in the middle oval. Write the
supporting details of your poem in the ovals clustered
around the topic. Supporting details can be thoughts,
ideas, descriptions, or anything you want.

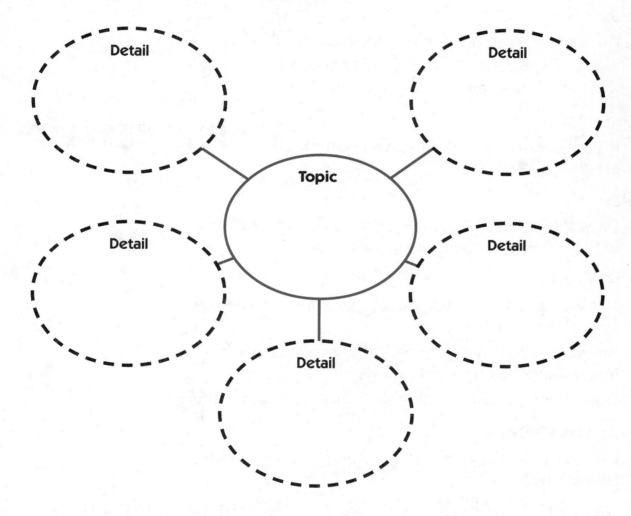

Drafting

Write your poem on a sheet of paper. Turn your ideas
into lines of poetry. Don't worry about rhyme or rhythm
patterns. If you wish, create other images with your
lines.

Name _____ Date _____

▶ **Writing a Free-Verse Poem**

Revising

Reread your free-verse poem. Make sure you feel good about it from start to finish. Use this checklist to help you revise your poem. Use proofreading marks to make changes.

Proofreading Marks	
∧	Add something.
ℓ	Take something out.
∼	Transpose.
sp	Check spelling.
⊙	Add a period.

Ideas

☐ Does your poem have one main focus or idea?

☐ Can you add more details so that the reader will get a better picture of your ideas?

Organization

☐ If you made a pattern, have you structured it precisely?

Voice

☐ Does the poem sound like you care or that you have definite feelings about the topic?

Word Choice

☐ Did you try to make use of comparisons such as metaphors and similes?

☐ Are your words precise so that your reader will understand exactly what you mean?

☐ Does every phrase and line say what you want it to say?

Sentence Fluency

☐ Do your lines flow smoothly, or do you need better transitions?

☐ Other __May include questions relating to adding ideas__ __and rewording for better effect.__

Mark your changes to the poem. If you made many changes, rewrite your poem. You may need to rewrite the poem several times to get it just how you want it.

Objective: Students revise their free-verse poems.

▶ **Writing a Free-Verse Poem**

Editing/Proofreading

Proofread your poem. Use this checklist to help you.

Conventions

☐ Does your poem have any spelling errors?

☐ Did you use capitalization in a consistent way?

☐ Did you use commas and end punctuation consistently?

☐ Did you use various types of pronouns correctly?

☐ Other **May include questions about grammar, usage, and mechanics specific to students' poems.**

Publishing

Use this checklist to get your poem ready for publishing.

Presentation

☐ Copy your poem onto a clean sheet of paper. You may want to use a special note card or decorated paper.

☐ Check for spelling and mechanics errors.

☐ Add any illustrations or decorations that you wish.

☐ Present your poem by using one of the following methods:
  • Place it in a collection of class poetry.
  • Place it in your writing portfolio.
  • Give it to the person for whom you wrote it.
  • Mail it to a magazine for a contest. **A number of magazines hold contests or print young people's original stories and poems.**
  • Share your poem by performing it. Read it to your class or another class.
  • Post your work on a poetry Web site for young people.
  • Keep it in your personal journal.

☐ Other **May include additional ways to present a poem.**

POETRY

Name _____ Date _____

Writing a Diamante

Objective: Students plan for the writing of a diamante.

Use the writing process to write a diamante.

Prewriting

Who is the audience for your diamante?

☐ Your teacher

☐ A family member

☐ A friend

☐ Your classmates

☐ Readers of a poetry magazine

☐ Club members

☐ Other **Audience should be specific.** _____

What is your purpose for writing your diamante?

☐ To describe a person, place, or thing

☐ To write a caption for a picture

☐ To add a poem to your portfolio

☐ To entertain someone

☐ Other **Purpose should be clearly stated.** _____

What is your topic?

Topic should be specific and will probably appear in the poem.

▶ **Writing a Diamante**

Write some ideas to describe your topic below.

_____ _____ _____

_____ _____ _____

_____ _____

Drafting

A diamante takes the shape of a diamond when it is completed. Fill in the blanks below to construct the lines of your diamante. Use your ideas from above. Change the wording of your ideas to match the forms that are required.

Line 1:

One noun (subject)   _____

Line 2:

Two adjectives   _____ _____

Line 3:

Three participles (-*ing* words)   _____ _____ _____

Line 4:

Four nouns   _____ _____ _____ _____

Line 5:

Three participles (-*ing* words)   _____ _____ _____

Line 6:

Two adjectives   _____ _____

Line 7:

Two nouns   _____ _____

POETRY

Name _____ Date _____

▶ **Writing a Diamante**

Objective: Students revise their diamante.

Revising

Reread your diamante. Use this checklist to help revise your poem. Use proofreading marks to make the changes.

Ideas

☐ Does your poem have just one idea?

☐ Are all the details related to your one idea?

Organization

☐ Does your poem have the correct number of words and lines?

☐ Does each line go with the line before and after it?

Voice

☐ Does the writing sound like *you?*

☐ Do your words bring the topic to life?

Word Choice

☐ Did you use each word as directed?

☐ Do you think any words need to be changed?

☐ Did you choose the most effective words you could think of?

Sentence Fluency

☐ Do your lines flow smoothly?

☐ Other ___**May include questions relating to changing**___
ideas and rewording for a better effect.

Write a revision if you have made many changes.

Proofreading Marks	
∧	Add something.
ℓ	Take something out.
∼	Transpose.
sp	Check spelling.
⊙	Add a period.

▶ **Writing a Diamante**

Editing/Proofreading

Proofread your diamante. Use this checklist to help you.

Conventions

☐ Does your poem have any spelling errors?

☐ Did you capitalize the beginning of each line?

☐ Did you use commas between words when necessary?

☐ Other **May include questions about grammar, usage, and mechanics specific to students' poems.**

Publishing

Use this checklist to get your poem ready for publishing.

Presentation

☐ Copy your poem onto a clean sheet of paper. You may want to use a special note card or decorated paper.

☐ Check for spelling and mechanics errors.

☐ Add any illustrations or decorations that you wish.

☐ Present your poem by using one of the following methods:
  • Combine art and poetry by creating a poster with your diamante and an illustration. Display it at school.
  • Place it in a collection of class poetry.
  • Place it in your writing portfolio.
  • Give it to the person for whom you wrote it.
  • Mail it to a magazine for a contest. **A number of magazines hold contests or print young people's original stories and poems.**
  • Share your poem by performing it. Read it to your class or another class.
  • Post your work on a poetry Web site for young people.
  • Keep it in your personal journal.

☐ Other **May include additional ways to present a poem.**

POETRY

Objective: Students plan for the writing of a persuasive poster.

Creating a Persuasive Poster

Use the writing process to create a persuasive poster.

Prewriting

Who is the audience for your persuasive poster?

☐ Your teacher

☐ Your class

☐ Your school **Poster could be displayed in the hall.**

☐ Your community

☐ Other __**Audience should be specific.**__

What is your purpose for creating a persuasive poster?

☐ You want to change the way people think about an issue.

☐ You want to change how people think *and* act regarding an issue.

☐ You want to point out a problem and convince others that the solution presented is the best way to solve the problem.

☐ Other __**Purpose should be clearly stated.**__

Describe the topic and specific aim of your persuasive poster.

Topic: __**The particular topic should be listed.**__

Aim: __**The particular aim or objective—what the writer wishes to accomplish regarding the topic—should be briefly described.**__

UNIT 4 Making a New Nation • **Lesson 1** *If You Lived at the Time of the*
American Revolution/Yankee Doodle

Objective: Students prewrite for a persuasive poster.

PERSUASIVE WRITING

▶ **Creating a Persuasive Poster**

**Plan the ideas for your persuasive poster. After doing
your research, use a web to organize your information.
State your topic, aim, and purpose in the center
rectangle. In the surrounding boxes, briefly list your
persuasive reasons. You do not need to fill in every box.**

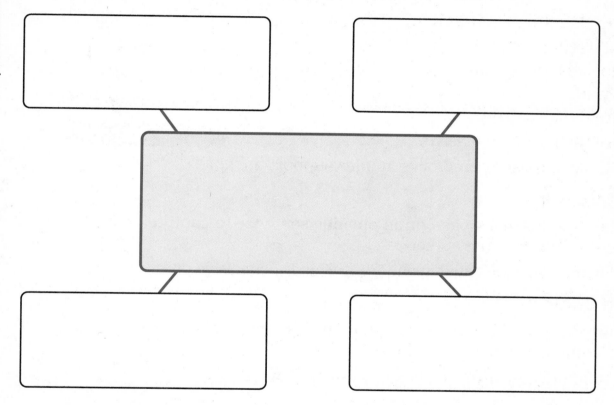

Drafting

**Use your web from above to create a mock-up of your
persuasive poster on a separate sheet of paper. Include
any rough design and illustration ideas.**

Creating a Persuasive Poster

Objective: Students revise their persuasive posters.

Revising

Evaluate your persuasive poster. Use this checklist to target areas for improvement. Use proofreading marks to make changes.

Ideas

☐ Are the ideas important to, and easily understood by, the audience?

☐ Does the design/illustration complement the ideas?

☐ Are the ideas compact?

☐ Are the ideas persuasive?

☐ Do facts, reasons, and/or examples support the goal?

Organization

☐ Have you used a slogan or an opening sentence to capture the attention of the audience?

☐ Could reasons be listed in a more logical or persuasive order?

Word Choice

☐ Have you used lively verbs and other descriptive words for maximum impact in the limited space?

☐ Could better words be chosen to stir the audience?

Sentence Fluency

☐ Can you improve the rhythm and flow of the writing?

Voice

☐ Does your poster show that *you* care about the message?

☐ Other <u>**May include any items or questions about**</u> **the ideas, organization, word choice, sentence fluency, or voice.**

Make all your changes to the poster mock-up. You may wish to draft a new version of your poster.

Proofreading Marks	
∧	Add something.
℮	Take something out.
⊂⊃	Close up space.
∧#	Add space.
⊙	Add a period.

▶ Creating a Persuasive Poster

Objective: Students edit and publish their persuasive posters.

P E R S U A S I V E   W R I T I N G

Editing/Proofreading

Carefully proofread your persuasive poster. Because of the increased size and visibility of posters, small mistakes can draw lots of attention to themselves. Use this checklist to make sure your poster is free of errors.

Conventions

☐ Are all proper names capitalized?

☐ Do all sentences contain and end with correct punctuation?

☐ Are there any spelling errors?

☐ Is verb tense consistent?

☐ Other **May include specific questions related to grammar, usage, and mechanics.**

Publishing

Use this checklist to get your persuasive poster ready to present.

Presentation

☐ Add bullets, stars, and other organizing features to help readers zero in on important information.

☐ Have another person evaluate your persuasive poster. Make any changes based on the suggestions you like.

☐ Neatly write your copy and add the final design and illustration elements to poster-sized paper or cardboard.

☐ Share your poster with your audience.

☐ Other **May describe any other way that students will be sharing their persuasive posters.**

UNIT 4 Making a New Nation • **Lesson 2** *The Night the Revolution Began*

Creating a Persuasive Flyer

Objective: Students prewrite for a persuasive flyer.

Use the writing process to create a persuasive flyer.

Prewriting

Who is the audience for your flyer?

☐ Your teacher

☐ Your class

☐ Your school

☐ Your community

☐ Other __Audience should be specific.__

What is your purpose for creating a flyer?

☐ You want to change the way people think about an issue.

☐ You want to change how people think *and* act regarding an issue.

☐ You want to point out a problem and convince others that the solution presented is the best way to solve the problem.

☐ Other __A general purpose should be stated.__

Describe the topic and specific aim of your flyer.

Topic: __The particular topic should be listed.__

Aim: __The particular aim or objective—what the writer wishes to accomplish regarding the topic—should be briefly described.__

UNIT 4 Making a New Nation • **Lesson 2** *The Night the Revolution Began*

 Creating a Persuasive Flyer

Plan the ideas for your persuasive flyer. After doing your research, use the web below to organize your information. State your topic, aim, and purpose in the center circle. On the four large branches, state your major persuasive points. List supporting facts, examples, and expert opinions on the smaller lines.

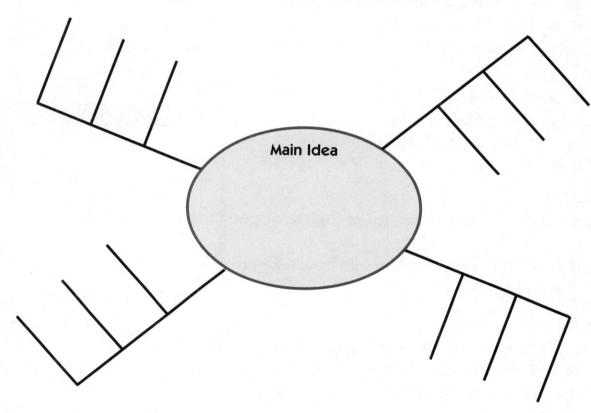

Main Idea

Drafting

Create a mock-up of your persuasive flyer. Include rough design and illustration ideas.

PERSUASIVE WRITING

UNIT 4   Making a New Nation • **Lesson 2** *The Night the Revolution Began*

▶ **Creating a Persuasive Flyer**

Objective: Students revise their persuasive flyer.

Revising

Evaluate your persuasive flyer. Use this checklist to target areas for improvement. Use proofreading marks to make changes.

Ideas

☐ Will the ideas be important to, and easily understood by, the audience?

☐ Does the design/illustration complement the ideas?

☐ Are the ideas compact?

☐ Have you used a slogan or an opening sentence to capture the attention of the audience?

Organization

☐ Could reasons be listed in a more logical or persuasive order?

☐ Could design/illustration elements be altered to better organize ideas?

Word Choice

☐ Have you used lively verbs, colorful adjectives, and other descriptive words for maximum impact?

☐ Could better words be chosen to stir the audience?

Sentence Fluency

☐ Can you improve the rhythm and flow of the writing?

Voice

☐ Does your poster show that you care about the message?

☐ Other **May include any items or questions about the ideas, organization, word choice, sentence fluency, or voice.**

Make all your changes to the flyer.

Proofreading Marks	
∧	Add something.
ℓ	Take something out.
⊃⊂	Close up space.
#	Add space.
⊙	Add a period.

Objective: Students edit and publish their persuasive flyer.

▶ **Creating a Persuasive Flyer**

Editing/Proofreading

Carefully proofread your persuasive flyer. If your flyer has mistakes, people may not take you seriously. Use this checklist to make sure your flyer is free of errors.

Conventions

☐ Are all proper names capitalized?

☐ Do all sentences contain and end with correct punctuation?

☐ Are there any spelling errors?

☐ Is verb tense consistent?

☐ Other **May include specific questions related to grammar, usage, and mechanics.**

Publishing

Use this checklist to get your flyer ready to present.

Presentation

☐ Have another person evaluate your flyer. Make any changes based on the suggestions you like.

☐ Add bullets, stars, and other organizing elements to help readers zero in on key information.

☐ Neatly write or type your copy onto a clean sheet of paper.

☐ Add design and illustration elements to make it visually appealing.

☐ Share your flyer with your audience.

☐ Other **May include other ideas for layout or formal presentation.**

PERSUASIVE WRITING

Name _____ Date _____

Writing a Persuasive Paragraph

Use the writing process to write a persuasive paragraph.

Prewriting

Who is the audience for your persuasive paragraph?

☐ Your teacher

☐ Your class

☐ Your family

☐ Readers of the school newspaper

☐ Other **Audience should be specific.** _____

What is your purpose for creating a persuasive paragraph?

☐ You want to change the way people think about an issue.

☐ You want to change how people think *and* act regarding an issue.

☐ You want to point out a problem and convince others that the solution presented is the best way to solve the problem.

☐ Other **A general purpose should be stated.** _____

Describe the topic and specific aim of your persuasive paragraph.

Topic: **The particular topic should be listed.** _____

Aim: **The particular aim or objective—what the writer wishes to accomplish regarding the topic—should be briefly described.**

PERSUASIVE WRITING

▶ **Writing a Persuasive Paragraph**

Plan the points of your persuasive paragraph. Write down what you want to include in each sentence.

1. Write the topic that states your viewpoint or describes a problem.	Have students describe the parts of their persuasive paragraphs. The persuasive paragraph should have a single controlling idea.
2. Write ideas for details to reinforce the viewpoint and to persuade readers.	Students may be able to fit up to three reasons within a single paragraph. Reasons should be connected to the topic.
3. Provide facts, examples, and/or expert opinions that support the viewpoint presented.	Students may wish to include each reason and related fact/example/expert opinion together in one sentence, or they may wish to give a reason and follow it up with a new sentence providing the fact/example/expert opinion.
4. Write ideas for making an emotional appeal to the audience.	For paragraphs that make an emotional appeal, students may rely more on examples and less on facts.

Drafting

Draft a persuasive paragraph on a sheet of paper. Turn your ideas into the topic sentence, reasons, and concluding sentence.

UNIT 4 Making a New Nation • **Lesson 3** *The Midnight Ride of Paul Revere*

Objective: Students revise their persuasive paragraphs.

▶ **Writing a Persuasive Paragraph**

Revising

Evaluate your persuasive paragraph. Use this checklist to pinpoint sentences that need improvement.

Ideas

☐ Does the opening sentence clearly state the viewpoint?

☐ Are the ideas or reasons clear?

☐ Are the ideas/reasons supported by facts, examples, or expert opinions so that they are logical and convincing?

☐ Is the aim limited to what can be accomplished in a single paragraph?

☐ Does a concluding sentence restate the viewpoint and/or ask for action?

Organization

☐ Could reasons be listed in a more logical or persuasive order?

Word Choice

☐ Have you used precise verbs and adjectives?

☐ Can you add any transition words to help readers better understand the ideas?

Sentence Fluency

☐ Would sentences read more smoothly if they were varied and expanded?

Voice

☐ Does your paragraph show a personal connection to the topic?

☐ Other **May include any items or questions about the ideas, organization, word choice, sentence fluency, or voice.**

Make all your changes to the draft.

Proofreading Marks

∧	Add something.
℮	Take something out.
⊂ ⊃	Close up space.
∧#	Add space.
⊙	Add a period.

Objective: Students edit and publish their persuasive paragraph.

PERSUASIVE WRITING

▶ **Writing a Persuasive Paragraph**

Editing/Proofreading

Carefully proofread your persuasive paragraph. Use this checklist to make sure your paragraph is free of mistakes.

Conventions

☐ Do all sentences contain the correct punctuation?

☐ Are there any words that are misused?

☐ Are there any spelling errors?

☐ Other **May include specific questions related to grammar, usage, and mechanics.**

Publishing

Use this checklist to get your persuasive paragraph ready to present.

Presentation

☐ Have another person read your persuasive paragraph. Make any changes based on suggestions you find helpful.

☐ Neatly rewrite or type your final version.

☐ Present your paragraph to your audience.

☐ Other **May include other ways to present, including adding items to make it more visually appealing and presenting it to the intended audience.**

Writing an Advertisement

Objective: Students plan to write an advertisement.

Use the writing process to produce an advertisement.

Prewriting

Who is the audience for your advertisement?

☐ Your teacher

☐ Your class **Advertisements could be**

☐ Your school **displayed in the hall.**

☐ Other ___ **Audience should be specific.** ___

What is your purpose for creating an advertisement?

☐ You want to convince others that a certain action will improve their lives.

☐ You want to persuade people to buy or use a certain product or service.

☐ Other **A general purpose should be stated.** ___

Describe the specific aim of your advertisement.
Students should describe in detail what they have selected to promote.

Select the techniques that will help you influence your audience.

☐ Appeal to reason **More than one may be checked, but**

☐ Appeal to the senses **students should plan on using one**

☐ Appeal to the emotions **approach and the related**

☐ Include one or more facts **techniques. For example an appeal**

☐ Include one or more examples **to reason might use facts and**

☐ Include one or more expert opinions **also an expert opinion. An appeal to the emotions might use examples.**

UNIT 4 Making a New Nation • **Lesson 4** *The Declaration of Independence*

PERSUASIVE WRITING

► **Writing an Advertisement**

Editing

Use the main-idea web to plan your advertisement. State your aim or objective in the center circle. On the four large branches, state your major persuasive points. List supporting facts, examples, expert opinions, and other specific information on the smaller horizontal lines. You do not need to use all lines.

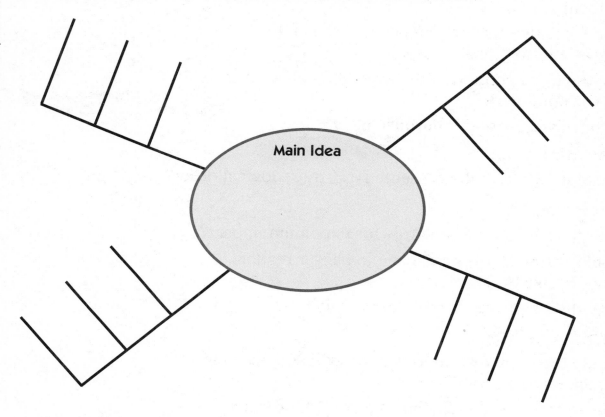

Main Idea

Drafting

Draft your advertising copy on a separate sheet of paper. Use your selected technique(s) to write it.

UNIT 4   Making a New Nation • **Lesson 4** *The Declaration of Independence*

▶ Writing an Advertisement

Revising

Evaluate your advertising copy. Use this checklist to target areas for improvement. Use proofreading marks to make changes.

Ideas

☐ Does an opening sentence or a featured element grab the reader?

☐ Does the advertisement appeal to reason, the senses, or emotions?

☐ Are the ideas supported by facts, examples, or expert opinions?

☐ Is the advertisement's purpose clear?

Organization

☐ Could information be presented in a more logical order?

Word Choice

☐ Have you used precise words for maximum impact?

☐ Could better words be chosen to trigger reader associations?

☐ Can ideas be phrased more creatively?

Sentence Fluency

☐ Would the copy read more smoothly if sentences were expanded and varied?

☐ Can you improve the rhythm and flow of the sentences used?

Voice

☐ Does your advertisement communicate your own excitement and interest in what is being promoted?

☐ Other **May include any items or questions about the ideas, organization, word choice, sentence fluency, or voice used in the advertisement.**

Make all of your changes to the advertisement.

Proofreading Marks	
∧	Add something.
ℓ	Take something out.
⊂⊃	Close up space.
#	Add space.
⊙	Add a period.

Objective: Students edit and publish their advertisement.

PERSUASIVE WRITING

▶ Writing an Advertisement

Editing/Proofreading

Carefully proofread your advertisement. Keep in mind that your audience will read it with a critical eye. Use this checklist to make sure your advertisement is free of mistakes.

Conventions

☐ Did you use correct capitalization and punctuation?

☐ Did you use comparatives and superlatives correctly?

☐ Are there any spelling errors?

☐ Do all subjects agree with their verbs?

☐ Check sentence structure and fix unintentional fragments and run-on or rambling sentences.

☐ Other **May include specific questions related to grammar, usage, and mechanics.**

Publishing

Use this checklist to get your advertisement ready to present.

Presentation

☐ Have another person read your advertisement. Make any changes based on suggestions you find helpful.

☐ Neatly rewrite your final version or type it on a computer.

☐ Add any formatting, design, and illustration features to make it more appealing. Elements such as bullets, stars, and other organizing features help readers zero in on key information. If you have access to a computer, you might want to create a visually appealing format using word processing or graphics software.

☐ Place your advertisement where your audience will view it.

☐ Other **May include other layout and illustration ideas. May include specific ways to present the advertisement to the audience.**

Writing a Letter to the Editor

Objective: Students prewrite for a letter to the editor.

Use the writing process to write a letter to the editor.

Prewriting

Who is the audience for your letter?

☐ Your teacher

☐ Your class

☐ Your school

☐ Your community **If the letter is intended to be more than**

☐ Other **an assignment for the teacher, the audience** **should be the readers of a publication.**

What is your purpose for writing a letter to the editor?

☐ You want to change the way people think about an issue.

☐ You want to change how people think *and* act regarding an issue.

☐ You want to point out a problem and convince others that the solution presented is the best way to solve the problem.

☐ Other **A general purpose should be stated.**

Describe the specific topic and goal of your letter to the editor.

The issue the writer wants to address should be listed.
Topic: _____

Aim: **The particular aim or objective—what the writer** **wishes to accomplish regarding the topic—should be** **briefly described.**

PERSUASIVE WRITING

▶ **Writing a Letter to the Editor**

Objective: Students continue to plan their letter to the editor.

Plan the points of your letter to the editor. Write down what you want to include.

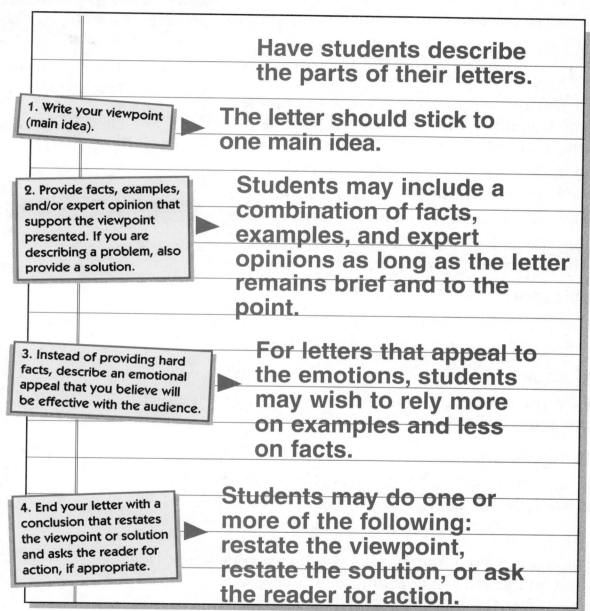

Have students describe the parts of their letters.

1. Write your viewpoint (main idea).

The letter should stick to one main idea.

2. Provide facts, examples, and/or expert opinion that support the viewpoint presented. If you are describing a problem, also provide a solution.

Students may include a combination of facts, examples, and expert opinions as long as the letter remains brief and to the point.

3. Instead of providing hard facts, describe an emotional appeal that you believe will be effective with the audience.

For letters that appeal to the emotions, students may wish to rely more on examples and less on facts.

4. End your letter with a conclusion that restates the viewpoint or solution and asks the reader for action, if appropriate.

Students may do one or more of the following: restate the viewpoint, restate the solution, or ask the reader for action.

Drafting

Draft a letter to the editor on a separate sheet of paper. Turn your prewriting ideas into the introduction, body, and conclusion of your letter.

UNIT 4 Making a New Nation • **Lesson 5** *The Master Spy of Yorktown*

▶ **Writing a Letter to the Editor**

Objective: Students revise their letters to the editor.

Revising

Evaluate your letter to the editor. Use this checklist to pinpoint areas for improvement.

Ideas

☐ Is your position on the topic clear?

☐ Are the ideas supported by facts, examples, or expert opinions (not just more of your own opinions) so that they are convincing?

☐ Do the ideas stick to the point, and is the letter content compact?

☐ Does each paragraph tell about only one idea?

☐ Does a conclusion restate the viewpoint or solution and, if appropriate, ask for action?

Organization

☐ Could reasons be listed in a more logical or persuasive order?

Word Choice

☐ Have you chosen precise verbs and other exact words for maximum impact?

Sentence Fluency

☐ Would the letter read more smoothly if sentences were expanded and varied?

Voice

☐ Think about your audience as you revise your letter. Does what you've written appeal to their concerns?

☐ Does the letter reflect *your* personal connection to the topic?

☐ Other **May include any items or questions about the ideas, organization, word choice, sentence fluency, or voice used in the letter.**

Make the changes to your letter to the editor.

Proofreading Marks

∧	Add something.
ℯ	Take something out.
⊂	Close up space.
⤒#	Add space.
⊙	Add a period.

UNIT 4 Making a New Nation • **Lesson 5** *The Master Spy of Yorktown*

Objective: Students edit and publish their letters to the editor.

▶ **Writing a Letter to the Editor**

Editing/Proofreading

Carefully proofread your letter to the editor. Use this checklist to make sure your letter is free of mistakes.

Conventions

☐ Make sure the format of the letter is correct.

☐ Check sentence structure and fix fragments and run-on or rambling sentences.

☐ Make sure the name of the publication and all proper names are capitalized and spelled correctly.

☐ Make sure that the inside address is correct.

☐ Make sure that sentences contain correct punctuation.

☐ Check for misused words and spelling errors.

☐ Other **May include specific questions related to grammar, usage, and mechanics.**

Publishing

Use this checklist to get your letter ready for publishing.

Presentation

☐ Have another person read your letter. Make any changes based on useful suggestions.

☐ Check the publication for specific instructions on submitting letters.

☐ Neatly rewrite, or correct and print, your final version.

☐ Sign your letter.

☐ Address the envelope.

☐ Proofread the envelope and your letter one more time.

☐ Get ready to mail your letter with the correct postage *or* give it to your reader.

☐ Other **May include suggestions for putting the letter on letterhead or posting it for a specific audience to read.**

PERSUASIVE WRITING

Writing a Persuasive Report

Use the writing process to write a persuasive report.

Prewriting

Who is the audience for your persuasive report?

☐ Your teacher

☐ Your class

☐ Your family

☐ Other __Audience should be specific.__

What is your purpose for writing a persuasive report?

☐ You want to change the way readers think about an issue.

☐ You want to change how readers think *and* act regarding an issue.

☐ You want to point out a problem and convince others that the solution presented is the best way to solve the problem.

☐ Other __A general purpose should be stated.__

Describe the aim or specific goal of your persuasive report. The student should describe the particular aim or objective—what he or she wishes to accomplish— regarding the selected topic.

Describe the opposing viewpoint. Just one opposing viewpoint should be described.

_____

_____

_____

Name _____   Date _____

UNIT 4   Making a New Nation • **Lessons 6 and 7**   *Shh! We're Writing the Constitution/We, the People of the United States*

Objective: Students organize their ideas for their persuasive report.

▶ **Writing a Persuasive Report**

Plan the structure of your persuasive report. In the topic rectangle, include both your topic and aim (specific goal). In the subtopic rectangles, include your major reasons or points. On the lines underneath, list at least two facts, examples, and/or expert opinions that you will use to defend your reasons.

Topic

[ ]

Subtopic   **Subtopic**

[ ]   [ ]

1. Have students describe the parts of their persuasive
2. reports. Every line does not have to be completed, but
   they should have two or more subtopics (major
3. reasons) under which are listed at least two items each.

Subtopic   **Subtopic**

[ ]   [ ]

1. _____   1. _____

2. _____   2. _____

3. _____   3. _____

Conclusion

[ ]

Drafting

Begin drafting your persuasive report, turning your prewriting ideas into paragraphs. Incorporate parallelism if possible.

UNIT 4 Making a New Nation • **Lessons 6 and 7** *Shh! We're Writing the Constitution/We, the People of the United States*

▶ **Writing a Persuasive Report**

Revising

Reread your persuasive report. Use this checklist to help you improve it.

Ideas

☐ Do you have an introduction that captures the attention of the audience?

☐ Will your main idea be clear to your audience?

☐ Are your reasons supported by facts, examples, or expert opinions?

☐ Did you include opposing ideas and then present evidence to argue against them?

☐ Do your reasons stick to the point?

☐ Is all your information accurate?

Organization

☐ Did you organize your supporting details in the best order to persuade your audience?

☐ Did you include topic sentences to present each new idea?

☐ Did you use transitions to help the reader move from one idea to the next?

Word Choice

☐ Have you chosen precise words that will help make the reader think or act in a certain way?

Sentence Fluency

☐ Are all your sentences easy to read and understand?

Voice

☐ Does the persuasive report reflect *your* personal connection to the topic?

☐ Other **May include any items or questions related to a persuasive report.**

Make the changes to your persuasive report.

Proofreading Marks	
∧	Add something.
℮	Take something out.
⊂⊃	Close up space.
⌃#	Add space.
⊙	Add a period.

Objective: Students edit and publish their persuasive report.

PERSUASIVE WRITING

Editing/Proofreading

Carefully proofread your persuasive report. Use this checklist to make sure it is free of mistakes.

Conventions

☐ Are all of your facts correct? Have you documented any sources you used? Have you given the proper credit to anyone else whose words you used?

☐ Are there any punctuation or capitalization errors?

☐ Are there any double negatives or other incorrect usage?

☐ Is verb tense consistent?

☐ Did you check sentence structure and fix unintentional fragments and run-on or rambling sentences?

☐ Other **May include specific questions related to grammar, usage, and mechanics.**

Publishing

Use this checklist to get your persuasive report ready to present.

Presentation

☐ Have another person read your persuasive report. Make any changes based on suggestions you find helpful.

☐ Neatly rewrite, or correct and print, your final copy. Make sure you have indented your paragraphs correctly.

☐ Make sure your report is neat and easy to read.

☐ Include any illustrations, charts, or diagrams that will back up your ideas.

☐ Share your report with your audience.

☐ Other **May include other ways of presenting and formatting issues, such as margins, page numbering, and binding. May include ways to share with specific audiences.**

UNIT 5 Going West • **Lesson I** *Sacagawea's Journey*

Writing a Dialogue Journal Response

Write a dialogue journal entry to record your response to your teacher's journal entry.

Write some ideas you can use in your dialogue journal response. You might want to tell about

- **how you agree or disagree with specific points**
- **how you feel about your teacher's response**
- **meanings you understood from the original literature selection**

Have students write ideas. These do not
need to be in complete sentences.

_____

Did your teacher's dialogue journal entry make you think of any questions for him or her? If so, write them below.

_____

_____

Write any other ideas about the original reading selection that you want to talk about.

_____

_____

- Using your ideas from above, write your response to your teacher's journal entry on a separate sheet of paper.
- When you have finished, check your entry. Make sure there are no mistakes. Make sure your entry tells all your ideas.

Name _____   Date _____

Writing in a Learning Log

Objective: Students plan to write a learning log entry.

Write a learning-log entry about one of your school subjects.

What school subject will you write about? _____
Answers should be specific.
_____

What is your purpose for writing about this subject?

☐ To help me remember what I read or what was discussed in class

☐ To help me understand by analyzing what I know

☐ To raise questions I have

☐ To remind myself that I want to learn more about a topic

☐ Other _____

Write some of your ideas for your entry here.

If students already know what they want to
write about—for example, if they only have
questions—they may go directly to the next
instruction.
_____
_____
_____
_____

Write your learning-log entry on a separate sheet of paper. When you have finished, check it to make sure that your ideas are clear and that you have included any necessary background information.

UNIT 5 Going West • **Lesson I** *Sacagawea's Journey*

Writing in a Learning Log

Objective: Students write questions for a learning-log question box.

Write a question-box entry to ask questions you have about a reading selection.

About what reading selection do you have questions?

Title: _____

Author: _____

Why are you writing your question-box entry?

☐ To learn more about a subject

☐ To understand more about a character

☐ To understand why a character behaved a certain way

☐ To understand what a word or phrase in the selection means

☐ Other _____

These examples are provided not only to help guide students in thinking of ideas for this assignment but also to help them better understand what they read in general.

Write your questions below. Write in complete sentences.

_____

_____

_____

Reread your questions. Make sure each question clearly states what you want to know.

PERSONAL WRITING

Objective: Students plan to write an entry in a literature response journal.

Writing a Literature Response Journal Entry

Write a response to a literature selection.

What literature selection will you respond to?

Title: _____

Author: __Selections may be fiction or nonfiction.__

Is there a particular focus for your journal entry?
Students may not have a focus yet.

Your response may take the form of a letter, dialogue, personal essay, or poem. Here are some ideas.
- a response to the author or to one of the characters
- a journal entry focusing on a certain part of the selection
- an imaginary dialogue with one of the characters
- a poem expressing a thought or feeling about the text
- a paragraph exploring your personal connection to your reading

Use exploratory freewriting about the reading selection to record your initial thoughts and feelings about it. Then review your freewriting and underline key ideas that you want to include in your response. Your freewriting can also be your response.

If you want to refine your ideas, write your literature-response journal entry on a separate sheet of paper.

Students may use freewriting to help them get ideas that they may then want to refine or narrow. Students' freewriting can also be the journal entry.

Objective: Students plan for an invitation.

Writing an Invitation

Work with your classmates to create an invitation asking an author of one of the literature selections in your book to come to speak to your class.

Prewriting

1. Who is the audience? Choose an author whose work everyone enjoyed and wanted to know more about. Include the title of the selection along with the author's name.

   Author: _**Responses should be the result of a democratic vote.**_

   Title: _____

2. What is the purpose for writing the invitation? **Students' answers may include that they wanted to know about the research behind the work or they wanted to learn more about the author.**

3. What will the format for the invitation be? **Answers may include a letter, a standard invitation, a drawing, or any acceptable creative format.**

4. Develop the body of the invitation with your classmates by answering the five *W*s. You should have answered *who?* and *why?* above.

   What? _____

   When? _____

   Where? _____

Drafting

Write your invitation on a separate sheet of paper. Include the answers to the questions above.

Writing a Thank-You Note

Write a thank-you note for some act of kindness someone did for you or your community.

Prewriting

Plan your thank-you note below.

Reason for note ▶	**Most thank-you notes start with the words "Thank you for . . ." Students should describe in detail what they are thankful for.**
Thoughts, feelings, other related information ▶	**Students may tell why the act of kindness was important to them.**
Conclusion ▶	**Students should include some kind of summary sentence. It could be a repetition of thanks or a nicety.**

Drafting

Write a draft of your thank-you note on a separate sheet of paper. Transfer your notes above directly to your draft. As you write, remember to think about your audience and the tone you want to convey.

Objective: Students prewrite for a thank-you note.

PERSONAL WRITING

Objective: Students revise, edit, and publish their thank-you notes.

▶ **Writing a Thank-You Note**

Revising

- ☐ Is the reason for writing your note clear?
- ☐ Do you have enough detail about the reason for your thanks?
- ☐ Would your sentences make more sense in another order?
- ☐ Are there other words you could use to express your feelings better?
- ☐ Do you sound sincere?
- ☐ Would you be happy to receive this note?
- ☐ Does each sentence lead to the next?

Proofreading Marks

¶	Indent.
∧	Add something.
ℓ	Take something out.
∼	Transpose.
≡	Make a capital letter.
sp	Check spelling.
⊙	Add a period.

Editing/Proofreading

- ☐ Are the name and address correct?
- ☐ Are there any spelling errors?
- ☐ Have you used capitalization and punctuation correctly, particularly in the address, salutation, and closing?

Publishing

- ☐ Type or write your thank-you note onto a clean sheet of paper.
- ☐ Reread it a final time for errors. Make sure you feel good about it.
- ☐ Sign your thank-you note at the bottom.
- ☐ Address the envelope and proofread it.
- ☐ Other **May include other questions about revising, editing, or publishing. You may want to read students' notes before they mail them.**

Writing an E-Mail Message

Write an e-mail message to your teacher.

Just because the message is electronic doesn't mean you ignore conventions. The tone and language of the message depend upon your audience and purpose for writing, just as it does in any type of writing. Politeness is also just as important in cyberspace as it is on paper. Think before sending your message. You don't want to write something you can't take back.

Plan what you will say in your e-mail.

What is your topic? This may be a reading selection to which you are responding. **Students should include the title and author of the selection.**

What ideas will you talk about? (You might want to refer to page 81 for help with ideas.) **Guide students to think about ideas for their literature response journals.**

Write your e-mail message using your computer program. Open a new e-mail message and fill in the boxes. First, fill in the correct e-mail address in the *To* box. Then, fill in the *Subject* box. Next, type your message body. Use your ideas from above. Don't forget to include a closing for your message.

After you have typed your message, check it for errors. Make sure you've included all the ideas you had in mind. Check your words to make sure your teacher would enjoy reading it and that your message is sincere.

Name _____ Date _____

Writing a Friendly Letter

Use the writing process to write a friendly letter.

Prewriting

Who is the audience for your friendly letter?

☐ Your teacher
☐ Your family
☐ A friend
☐ Other _____ **Audience should be specific.** _____

What is your purpose for writing?

☐ To tell someone about a specific thing that has happened
☐ To tell about what has been happening in your life
☐ To tell someone about some news
☐ To let someone know you are thinking about him or her
☐ To share an exciting adventure you had with someone
☐ Other **Purpose should be clearly stated.** _____

Write the name and address of the person you will write to below.

Name: _____

Address: _____

City: _____ State: _____ Zip Code: _____

UNIT 5 Going West • **Lesson 3** *The Journal of Wong Ming-Chung*

▶ Writing a Friendly Letter

Objective: Students plan their topics for their friendly letter.

PERSONAL WRITING

Plan your friendly letter by writing what you will include in it. Students should write ideas for each paragraph of the body of their letter.

Start with a greeting that introduces your letter.
▶ Students should greet their recipient with a phrase such as "It's been a long time since we talked."

Share news about your life or introduce the topic you are writing about.
▶ Students can just write down brief ideas to help them compose sentences later.

Write other items of interest or details about the one topic you chose.
▶ Students should not jump around between ideas. If a student is answering a letter that has been written to him or her, other ideas would include any topics asked about in the letter.

Wrap up your letter with some final thoughts.
▶ Students should write ideas to conclude the letter.

Drafting

Write your letter on a separate sheet of paper. Use the topics you listed above as main ideas. Be sure to add the heading, salutation, and closing. In the body, you can make each main idea a paragraph. You might want to ask the reader questions as you go.

Name _____ Date _____

► **Writing a Friendly Letter**

Objective: Students revise their friendly letters to make sure they make sense and include all their ideas.

Revising

Reread your letter. Use the checklist below to help you improve it.

Ideas
☐ Have you included important details about the topics you wrote about?
☐ Will your reader find your topics interesting?
☐ Did you include a closing to wrap up your letter?

Organization
☐ Does each new paragraph express a new idea?
☐ Does each paragraph tell about only one topic?
☐ Does the order of your paragraphs make sense?

Voice
☐ Did you express yourself in a friendly way, or is your tone too formal?
☐ Does your letter sound like you really wanted to write it?
☐ Does your letter show your enthusiasm for your topics?

Word Choice
☐ Do your words express what you mean? Have you chosen words that show why an event was funny, happy, sad, or boring?
☐ Have you used transition words to connect your topics?

Sentence Fluency
☐ Are your sentences smooth and easy to read?
☐ Are your sentences interesting? Do they differ from one another?

Other   May include questions relating to adding
☐ information, cutting information, rewriting parts, or
reordering parts.

Mark any revisions on your letter. If you have a lot of changes, rewrite your letter.

Proofreading Marks

⊬ Indent.
∧ Add something.
⌿ Take something out.
∼ Transpose.
sp ◯ Check spelling.
⊙ Add a period.

UNIT 5 Going West • **Lesson 3** *The Journal of Wong Ming-Chung*

Objective: Students get their friendly letters ready for mailing.

Editing/Proofreading

Proofread your letter. Make sure your letter will make a good impression on your reader. Use this checklist to make sure you remember everything.

Conventions

☐ Are the name and address correct?

☐ Does each sentence have the correct capitalization and punctuation?

☐ Did you use commas correctly?

☐ Did you check for spelling errors, including those missed by a spell checker?

☐ Have you followed the correct format for a friendly letter?

☐ Other **May include questions about grammar, usage, and mechanics related to a friendly letter.**

Publishing

Use this checklist to get your letter ready for publishing.

Presentation

☐ Write your letter on a clean sheet of paper.

☐ Check your letter again for any errors. Make sure you copied all of the parts of the letter.

☐ Sign your letter.

☐ Fold your letter. Add any drawings or pictures that you wrote you were enclosing.

☐ Address the envelope and proofread it.

☐ Place the correct postage on the envelope and mail it. **You may want to have students turn in their letters before mailing. You can assess them and hand back the letters for mailing.**

Writing a Letter of Concern

Use the writing process to write a business letter of concern.

Prewriting

Who is the audience for your letter of concern?

☐ An organization ___**Name of the organization**___

☐ A professional person ___**Name and title of the person**___

☐ A company or store ___**Name of the company or store**___

☐ A government official ___**Name and title of the person**___

☐ Other ___**Audience should be specific. Students' answers may include more specific organizations such as**___

What is your purpose for writing? **the school board, a civic**

☐ To share your thoughts about an environmental issue **group, or the**

☐ To express concern over a safety issue **president of the United**

☐ To give a suggestion ___**Name of suggestion**___ **States.**

☐ To express strong feelings about something ___**What the issue is**___

☐ Other ___**Purpose should be clearly stated and specific.**___

Write the name and address of the person to whom you will write.

Name: _____

Address: _____

City: _____ State: _____ Zip Code: _____

Help students research the name and address of the person to whom they plan to write.

Objective: Students determine the audience and purpose for a letter of concern.

UNIT 5 Going West • **Lesson 4** *The Coming of the Long Knives*

> **Writing a Letter of Concern**

Objective: Students plan the body of a letter of concern according to the audience and purpose they chose.

Plan the body of your letter by writing down what you will include in each paragraph. Remember that in a business letter, the focus should be on the reader.

Give the reason for writing. ▶	**Students should describe the issue or situation and give their opinion.**
Explain how you would correct the problem or change the situation. ▶	**Students should write realistic ideas.**
Explain how your solution will work. ▶	**Students should provide facts or examples to back up their ideas.**
Conclusion ▶	**Students should ask that action be taken to change the situation. They may want to summarize their arguments or tell how they will follow up.**

Drafting

Write a draft of your letter on a separate sheet of paper. Turn your ideas into paragraphs. Start a new paragraph for each new idea. Be sure that you use a tone that will make your reader take you seriously. Add the heading, inside address, salutation, and closing.

UNIT 5 Going West • **Lesson 4** *The Coming of the Long Knives*

Objective: Students revise their letters of concern.

> **Writing a Letter of Concern**

Revising

Reread your letter. Use this checklist to improve it.

Ideas

☐ Is your purpose clearly stated at the beginning?

☐ Do you back up your ideas with facts or examples?

☐ Did you offer a valid solution?

Organization

☐ Does the order of your paragraphs make sense?

☐ Does each paragraph contain a different idea?

Voice

☐ Does your letter sound businesslike?

☐ Does your writing show that you truly care about your topic?

Word Choice

☐ Does your letter sound courteous? Your audience will be more likely to take action if you have been polite.

☐ Will your words tell the reader exactly what you mean? Did you use precise nouns, verbs, adjectives, and adverbs?

Sentence Fluency

☐ Are your sentences smooth and easy to read?

☐ Do the lengths of your sentences vary?

Other

☐ May include questions relating to adding information, cutting information, rewriting parts, or reordering parts.

Write your revisions on your letter. Add anything else that you think it needs to get your point across. If you have made many changes, rewrite your letter on another piece of paper.

Proofreading Marks	
⊬	Indent.
∧	Add something.
ℓ	Take something out.
∼	Transpose.
⊝	Check spelling.
⊙	Add a period.

▶ **Writing a Letter of Concern**

Editing/Proofreading

PERSONAL WRITING

Proofread your letter. If you want your reader to act, you want to make a good impression. Use this checklist to make sure you remember everything.

Conventions

☐ Did you use the correct spacing between the different parts of the letter?

☐ Did you capitalize names of streets, cities, months, and people?

☐ Did you capitalize the title of the recipient and the organization or company in the inside address?

☐ Did you capitalize the word *Dear*, all nouns in the salutation, and the first word of the closing?

☐ Did you use commas correctly in the address and closing?

☐ Did you check for spelling errors?

☐ Other **May include questions about grammar, usage, and mechanics related to a business letter.**

Publishing

Use this checklist to get your letter ready for publishing.

Presentation

You may want to discuss conventions for signing business letters.

☐ Write your letter on a clean sheet of paper. Use only one side of the page. You may want to type and print your letter. Leave space between your closing and your name so that you can sign the letter.

☐ Reread your letter and correct any final errors.

☐ Sign your letter.

☐ Address and proofread the envelope. Put the person's name and title on the envelope.

☐ Fold the letter and place it in the envelope.

☐ Other **You may want to read students' letters before they mail them.**

Objective: Students determine the audience and purpose for a friendly letter.

UNIT 5 Going West • **Lesson 5** *Old Yeller and the Bear*

Writing a Friendly Letter

Use the writing process to write a friendly letter describing what happened in a story you read.

Prewriting

Who is the audience for your friendly letter?

☐ Your teacher

☐ Your family

☐ A friend

☐ Other _____ **Students' answers may include the following: My best friend, a parent, a classmate, or a**

What is your purpose for writing? **specific person.**

☐ To convince someone to read an interesting story

☐ To make someone's day happier

☐ To tell someone how excited you are when you read things you like

☐ Other _____ **Purpose should be clearly stated.** _____

Write the name and address of the person you will write to below.

Name: _____

Address: _____

City: _____ State: _____ Zip Code: _____

Name _____ Date _____

Objective: Students plan their topics for their friendly letters.

P E R S O N A L   W R I T I N G

Plan your friendly letter by writing what you will include in it. Students should write ideas for each paragraph of the body of the letter.

Start with an opening that introduces your letter.	▶ Students can tell the reader why they are writing this letter.
Tell the topic you are writing about.	▶ Students can write down brief ideas to help them compose sentences later. This may be the title and author of the book or story they have read.
Write details about the one topic you chose.	▶ Students should give the plot details and tell what they think of the details. If students are having trouble, you may want to have them use a character web or plot-line diagram to help them analyze the story.
Wrap up your letter with some final thoughts.	▶ Students should write ideas to conclude the letter.

Drafting

Write your letter on a separate sheet of paper. Use the topics you listed above as main ideas. Be sure to add the heading, salutation, and closing. In the body, make each idea a paragraph.

Objective: Students revise their friendly letters to make sure they make sense and include all their ideas.

▶ **Writing a Friendly Letter**

Revising

Reread your letter. Use this checklist to help you improve it.

Ideas

☐ Have you told the reader why you are writing?

☐ Have you included important details about your topic? Have you left anything out so that your reader might be confused?

☐ Will your reader find your details interesting?

☐ Did you give your opinion (perhaps why you liked the story or why you liked certain things that happened)?

☐ Did you include a closing to wrap up your letter?

Organization

☐ Does each new paragraph express a new idea?

☐ Does each paragraph tell about only one topic?

☐ Does the order of your paragraphs make sense?

Voice

☐ Does your letter sound like you really wanted to write it?

☐ Does your letter show your enthusiasm for your topic?

Word Choice

☐ Have you chosen words that show why an event was funny, happy, sad, or boring?

☐ Have you used transition words to connect your topics?

Sentence Fluency

☐ Are your sentences smooth and easy to read?

Other   **May include questions relating to any of the above areas.**

☐ _____

Mark any revisions on your letter.

Proofreading Marks	
¶	Indent.
∧	Add something.
ℓ	Take something out.
∼	Transpose.
sp	Check spelling.
⊙	Add a period.

▶ **Writing a Friendly Letter**

Editing/Proofreading

Proofread your letter. Make sure you make a good impression on your reader. Use this checklist to make sure you remembered everything.

Conventions

- ☐ Are the name and address correct?
- ☐ Does each sentence have the correct capitalization and punctuation?
- ☐ Did you use commas correctly?
- ☐ Are there any spelling errors?
- ☐ Have you followed the correct format for a friendly letter?
- ☐ Other **May include questions about grammar, usage, and mechanics related to a friendly letter.**

Publishing

Use this checklist to get your letter ready for publishing.

Presentation

- ☐ Write your letter on a clean sheet of paper.
- ☐ Check the letter for any errors. Make sure you copied all the parts of your letter.
- ☐ Sign your letter.
- ☐ Fold your letter.
- ☐ Address the envelope and proofread it.
- ☐ Place the correct postage on the envelope and mail it.

You may want to have students turn in their letters before mailing. You can assess them and hand back the letters for mailing.

Objective: Students get their friendly letters ready for mailing.

PERSONAL WRITING

Name _____ Date _____

Writing a Letter of Request

Objective: Students determine the audience and purpose for a letter of request.

Use the writing process to write a business letter of request.

Prewriting

Who is the audience for your letter of request? **Name of the**

☐ An organization or company **organization or company**

☐ A professional person **Name and title of the person**

☐ Other **Audience should be specific. Students' answers may include schools, government agencies, or**
What is your purpose for writing? **famous people.**

☐ To find information for a report

☐ To check facts for a report

☐ To find out what resources are available on a topic

☐ To find information for a visit to a place

☐ Other **Purpose should be clearly stated. Students' answers may include: to ask about the policy of a company, to check out the statistics of a sports team**
Write the name and address of the person you will **or player, or to**
write to below. **find out about the availability of a product.**

Name: _____

Address: _____

City: _____ State: _____ Zip Code: _____

UNIT 5 Going West • **Lesson 6** *Bill Pickett: Rodeo-Ridin' Cowboy*

▶ **Writing a Letter of Request**

Plan the body of your letter by writing down what you will include in each paragraph.

Objective: Students plan the body of a letter of request.

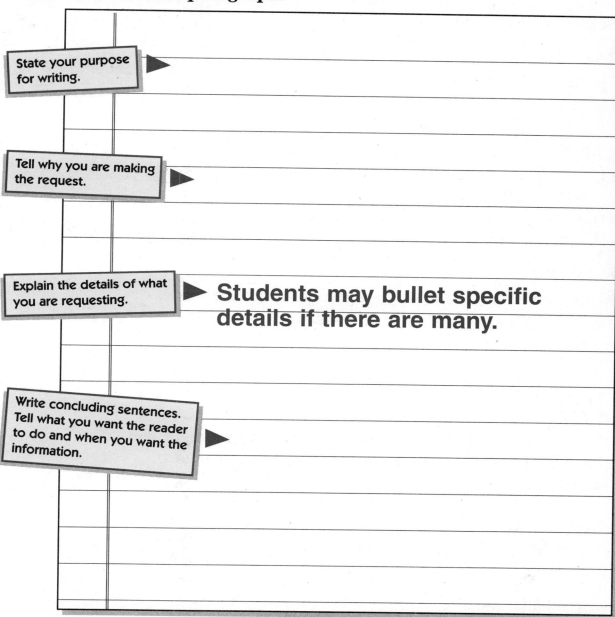

State your purpose for writing.

Tell why you are making the request.

Explain the details of what you are requesting. ▶ **Students may bullet specific details if there are many.**

Write concluding sentences. Tell what you want the reader to do and when you want the information.

PERSONAL WRITING

Drafting

Write your letter of request on a separate sheet of paper. Turn the information above into paragraphs. Add the rest of the parts of a business letter.

Objective: Students revise their letters of request.

UNIT 5 Going West • **Lesson 6** *Bill Pickett: Rodeo-Ridin' Cowboy*

▶ **Writing a Letter of Request**

Revising

Reread your letter. Use the following checklist to help you.

Ideas

☐ Is your request stated clearly in the first sentence?

☐ Did you explain why you want the information?

☐ Do you provide enough details about what you are requesting?

☐ Did you state clearly what action you want the reader to take?

Organization

☐ Does the arrangement of your paragraphs make sense?

☐ Does each paragraph stick to one subject?

Voice

☐ Is your letter polite and businesslike?

Word Choice

☐ Do you need to change any words so that your reader will want to respond to your request? (Example: Change *I want you to send me . . .* to *I would appreciate it if you would send me . . .*)

☐ Do you need to change any words to be more specific about what you are requesting?

Sentence Fluency

☐ Are your sentences smooth and easy to read?

Other

☐ **May include questions related to the specifics of the request.**

Make all of your changes to your letter. Add anything else you think your letter needs.

Proofreading Marks	
¶	Indent.
∧	Add something.
ℓ	Take something out.
∾	Transpose.
sp⊙	Check spelling.
⊙	Add a period.

Objective: Students get their letters of request ready for mailing.

PERSONAL WRITING

▶ **Writing a Letter of Request**

Editing/Proofreading

Proofread your letter. Letters with mistakes do not make a good impression. Use this checklist to help you.

Conventions

☐ Did you follow the correct format for writing a business letter?

☐ Did you capitalize names of streets, cities, months, and people?

☐ Did you capitalize the title of the recipient and the company in the inside address?

☐ Did you capitalize the word *Dear*, all nouns in the salutation, and the first word of the closing?

☐ Did you check for spelling errors, including those missed by a spell checker?

☐ Other **May include questions about grammar**, usage, **and mechanics related to a business letter.**

Publishing

Use this checklist to get your letter ready to mail.

Presentation **You may want to discuss conventions for signing business letters.**

☐ Write your letter on a clean sheet of paper. Use only one side of the page. You may want to type and print your letter. Leave space between your closing and your name so that you can sign the letter.

☐ Reread your letter again for errors.

☐ Sign your letter.

☐ Address and proofread the envelope. Put the person's name and title on the envelope.

☐ Fold the letter and place it in the envelope. Put the correct postage on the envelope and mail it.

☐ Other **You may want to read students' letters before they mail them.**

Objective: Students determine the audience and purpose for a memo.

Writing a Memo

Write a memo to a person or several people.

Prewriting

Who is the audience for your memo?

☐ Your teammates

☐ Your classmates

☐ Families of the students in your school

☐ A person within an organization

☐ Other **Audience should be specific. Students may** **choose to imagine that they are in the business**

What is your purpose for writing? **world or are a government**

☐ To tell someone about a meeting **employee, such as the**

☐ To explain a procedure or give instructions **president of the U.S.**

☐ To ask for donations of items to be used in the classroom

☐ Other **Purpose should be clearly stated.**

Report
due Friday

Writing a Memo • **Writer's Workbook**

UNIT 5 Going West • **Lesson 7** *McBroom the Rainmaker*

▶ **Writing a Memo**

PERSONAL WRITING

Objective: Students plan the body of a memo specific to the audience and purpose they chose.

Plan the body of your memo by writing down what you will include in each section.

State your reason for writing and your main point. ▶

Provide all the details that explain or support your subject. ▶

Identify follow-up action that needs to be taken. Include positive results that you expect.

▶ Positive results can be as simple as *Hope to see you there!*

Drafting

Write a draft of your memo on a separate sheet of paper. Add the information for the heading. Turn the details from above into short paragraphs.

Name _____ Date _____

Objective: Students revise the memo they drafted.

▶ **Writing a Memo**

Revising

Reread your memo. Make sure it communicates the correct information. Use the checklist below to help you. Use proofreading marks to make the changes.

Ideas

☐ Is the purpose clear?

☐ Did you limit the memo to one main point and two or three related points?

☐ Do your details explain or support your subject?

☐ Have you told the reader whether any action is required?

Organization

☐ Did you include clear information in the heading?

☐ Are the details organized so that they are easy to follow?

Voice

☐ Do you sound confident?

Word Choice

☐ Are your words polite and businesslike?

☐ Are you encouraging, even if you must point out a problem?

☐ Do you use exact words when discussing details?

☐ Were you as brief as possible?

Sentence Fluency

☐ Are your sentences smooth and easy to read?

☐ Did you include transitions from one sentence to the next?

Other

☐ **May include questions related to a memo.**

Mark your changes on your memo. Add anything else you think your memo needs.

Proofreading Marks

¶   Indent.

∧   Add something.

℘   Take something out.

∼   Transpose.

sp   Check spelling.

⊙   Add a period.

PERSONAL WRITING

▶ **Writing a Memo**

Editing/Proofreading

Proofread your memo. Use this checklist to make sure you remembered everything.

Conventions

☐ Does your letter follow the correct format for writing a memo?

☐ Did you capitalize proper nouns, including names of departments and titles of people?

☐ Did you check for spelling errors, including those missed by a spell checker?

☐ Other **May include questions about conventions specific to a memo, such as spacing.**

Publishing

Use this checklist to get your memo ready to present.

Presentation

☐ Rewrite your memo on a clean sheet of paper. If you have access to a computer, use a word processing program to type your memo and then print it.

☐ Reread your memo and check for errors. Check for proper spacing. Make any necessary corrections.

☐ If you typed your memo, initial it after your name.

☐ Make copies of your memo for everyone who needs one.

☐ Hand your memo to your audience or place one in each recipient's mailbox.

☐ Other **May include additional items for presentation, including the addition of graphics.**

Writing a Personal Narrative

Objective: Students plan the audience and purpose for a personal narrative.

Use the writing process to write a personal narrative.

Prewriting

Who is the audience for your personal narrative?

☐ Your teacher

☐ Your family

☐ A close friend

☐ Magazine readers

☐ Other **Audience should be specific.** _____

What is your purpose for writing?

☐ To share an important event

☐ To help your audience learn a lesson from an experience you had

☐ To help you remember something that happened to you

☐ Other **Purpose should be clearly stated. Students may be writing about a person that influenced them or**

What event will you write about? **did something special for them. They will still be**

writing
_____ **about an**

event or
Does your audience know anything about the event you **events in**

will write about? _____ **their lives.**

If you answered no, make sure you explain clearly the events and people involved.

UNIT 6 Journeys and Quests • **Lesson 1** *The Story of Jumping Mouse*

► Writing a Personal Narrative

Objective: Students organize their thoughts about a person or event before writing a personal narrative.

Complete the chain-of-events chart to show what events happened. Start with the first thing you want to tell. Then tell what it led to. Complete the chart by thinking of the outcomes of each event. Include your feelings as events.

Make sure students include events that lead from one to the other. This will help tie the different events together. Students may include how an event or action made them feel.

Students may wish to complete a story map instead. Allow students to select the graphic organizer they think will be the most helpful.

Drafting

Write your personal narrative on a sheet of paper using the chain-of-events chart above. Provide details so the reader can understand and share your experiences. Tell how the events made you feel.

▶ **Writing a Personal Narrative**

Objective: Students revise their personal narrative.

Revising

Reread your personal narrative. Use this checklist to help you improve it.

Ideas

☐ Did you provide enough background details for your audience?

☐ Have you told how the events made you feel?

☐ Do all the details and events relate to your main focus?

☐ Will your audience feel that your story is complete?

☐ Do you present your story in an interesting way? Will the reader want to keep reading until the end?

Organization

☐ Do all of your events follow one another in a logical order?

☐ Do you use transitions effectively to move the narrative story forward in time?

Voice

☐ Does your narrative sound like you?

Word Choice

☐ Did you use precise details so that your audience can imagine exactly how the events happened?

Sentence Fluency

☐ Did you use different kinds of sentences?

☐ Other **May include any new ideas or additional questions pertaining to a personal narrative.**

Write your revisions on your paper. If you have made many changes, rewrite your narrative on another sheet of paper.

Proofreading Marks	
∧	Add something.
ℓ	Take something out.
≡	Make a capital letter.
sp ⟲	Check spelling.
⊙	Add a period.

UNIT 6 Journeys and Quests • **Lesson I** *The Story of Jumping Mouse*

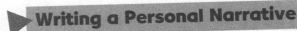
Writing a Personal Narrative

NARRATIVE WRITING

Objective: Students edit and publish their personal narrative.

Editing/Proofreading

Proofread your personal narrative. Careless mistakes can confuse your audience and take away from the story line. Use this checklist to help you remember everything.

Conventions

☐ Did you use the correct spelling, including personal names?

☐ Does each sentence have the correct punctuation?

☐ Did you use quotations with dialogue correctly?

☐ Have you written the correct form of plural nouns?

☐ Do all of your subjects and verbs agree?

☐ Other **May include other questions about grammar, usage, and mechanics, such as capitalization of the word *I*.**

Publishing

Use this checklist to get your narrative ready for publishing.

Presentation

☐ Rewrite your narrative onto a clean sheet of paper, or type it on a computer.

☐ Read your narrative for any final errors.

☐ If you wish, illustrate an event or person from your narrative.

☐ Present your description by using one of the following methods.

  ▶ Put your story into a book format by creating a cover for it.

  ▶ Give an oral presentation of your narrative.

  ▶ Publish your story electronically.

  ▶ Send it to a magazine that publishes student writing.

  ▶ Place it in your Writing Portfolio.

Writing a Biography

Objective: Students plan the audience and purpose for a biography.

Use the writing process to write a story about someone's life.

Prewriting

Who is the audience for your biography?

☐ Your classmates

☐ Your family

☐ Your teacher

☐ Readers of the school newspaper

☐ Patrons at the library

☐ Other **Audience should be specific.** _____

What is your purpose for writing?

☐ To tell about a person's good deeds

☐ To explain why you admire someone

☐ To learn more about someone

☐ Other **Purpose should be clearly stated. Students' answers may include to convince others of the merits of this person, to teach the class about a historical figure, or to display information in the library.**

Who will you write about? _____

Does your audience already know something about this person? _____

If so, you may be able to skip telling certain things about him or her.

You will need to conduct research about this person. On a piece of paper, list some questions you would like to answer as you research this person.

UNIT 6 Journeys and Quests • **Lesson 2** *Trapped by the Ice!*

▶ **Writing a Biography**

Objective: Students complete a time line to organize events for a biography.

Complete the time line to help you organize your biography. As you do your research, insert events or other important information in order. Include interesting information about your subject's life.

Subject of Time Line _____

Date: Event:

Allow students time to conduct research. They may or may not transfer their information directly to the time line. If students are simply taking notes first, make sure they transfer the information to the time line in time order. Students may wish to interview their subject if he or she is not a historical figure and is known to the student.

Drafting

Write your biography on a sheet of paper. Be sure to give details in time order.

▶ **Writing a Biography**

Objective: Students revise their biography.

Revising

Read your biography. Use this checklist to improve your biography.

Ideas

☐ Does your opening state your focus?

☐ Are events in the person's life told accurately?

☐ Did you use details from your sources to support your ideas?

☐ Did you describe the person in an interesting way?

☐ Did you include background information to give readers the full story?

☐ Do you have an effective beginning and closing?

Organization

☐ Did you tell about events in a specific order?

☐ Did you include transitions from one idea to the next?

☐ Do you have topic sentences to introduce new ideas?

Voice

☐ Will your writing make your audience care about the subject?

Word Choice

☐ Did you use vivid details to make the events of your subject's life seem real?

☐ Do your words say exactly what you mean?

Sentence Fluency

☐ Are your sentences smooth and easy to read?

☐ Can you vary any sentences if the structure is repeated?

☐ Other **May include questions specifically related to revising a biography.**

Make your changes to your biography. If you have made many changes, write a revision.

Proofreading Marks	
ℰ	Take something out.
∼	Transpose.
⟋sp⟍	Check spelling.
⊙	Add a period.

NARRATIVE WRITING

▶ **Writing a Biography**

Editing/Proofreading

Read your biography. Use the checklist below to help you check it for errors. Use editing marks to make changes.

Conventions

☐ Did you use the correct spelling, including personal names?

☐ Are all of your details about the person's life correct? Be sure to check dates, special names, and place names.

☐ Does each sentence have the correct punctuation?

☐ Other **May include other questions about grammar, usage, and mechanics related to a biography.**

Publishing

Use this checklist to get your biography ready for publishing.

Presentation

☐ Write your biography on a clean sheet of paper. If possible, use a computer to type it.

☐ Check for any errors on your final copy.

☐ Find a photo or illustration of the person and attach it to your writing.

☐ Publish your biography by using one of the following methods.

  ▶ Read it to your class.
  ▶ Post it by putting it on the classroom, school, or library bulletin board.
  ▶ Give it to the editor of your school newspaper.
  ▶ Share it with your family.
  ▶ Place it in your Writing Portfolio.

Proofreading Marks	
¶	Indent.
∧	Add something.
ℓ	Take something out.
∼	Transpose.
≡	Make a capital letter.
sp◯	Check spelling.
⊙	Add a period.

Objective: Students edit and publish their biography.

Writing a Play

Objective: Students plan the audience and purpose for a play.

Use the writing process to write a play.

Prewriting

Who is the audience for your play?

☐ Classmates

☐ Families of your schoolmates

☐ A scouting group or other organization

☐ Your friends

☐ Other **Audience should be specific.** _____

What is your purpose for writing?

☐ To entertain your audience

☐ To teach your audience about a subject or event

☐ To teach a moral or lesson about an experience.

☐ Other **Purpose should be clearly stated.** _____

Plan your characters using the chart below.

Name	Age	Appearance	Personality Traits

Students should complete as many rows as they like. Encourage students to think about what the characters will be like before they write. If students are rewriting a literature selection, they may not need to fill in the chart completely. You may wish to have students write their plays in groups.

UNIT 6 Journeys and Quests • **Lesson 3** *Apollo 11: First Moon Landing*

▶ **Writing a Play**

Objective: Students plan the story line of a play and write a draft of it.

Plan the plot of your play. This will help you outline the main scenes.

> **Title**

> **Conflict**

> **Key Events**

> **Students should tell what happens at the beginning of the play, the major conflict, and the resolution.**

> **Resolution**

Drafting

Write your play on separate paper. Begin by giving the cast of characters and the setting of the play. Include any stage directions and directions for how a character should act or speak. Develop your characters as the action in the play moves along.

Journeys and Quests • **Lesson 3** *Apollo 11: First Moon Landing*

Objective: Students revise their plays.

Revising

Read your play. Imagine someone listening and watching a performance of your play. Use the checklist below to help you revise it.

Ideas

☐ Do your dialogue and stage directions show clearly what happens in your play?

☐ Did you include details that make your characters believable?

☐ Does the audience find out about characters gradually through the dialogue and action?

Organization

☐ Does your play begin with a title, description of characters, and an explanation of the setting?

☐ Does your play have a beginning, middle, and end?

☐ Do the stage directions go with the action and dialogue?

Voice

☐ Does the play sound as if you wrote it rather than someone else?

Word Choice

☐ Does the dialogue of the characters show their personalities?

☐ Do your stage directions tell exactly what you want to see or how the actors should perform?

Sentence Fluency

☐ Is your dialogue written the way the characters would actually speak? Did you use fragments?

☐ Other __**May include specific questions related to**__ **dialogue, stage directions, plot, characters, and so on.**

Make changes to your play. Add anything else you think your play needs.

Proofreading Marks	
∧	Add something.
ℓ	Take something out.
∿	Transpose.
≡	Make a capital letter.
sp	Check spelling.
⊙	Add a period.

▶ **Writing a Play**

NARRATIVE WRITING

Objective: Students edit and present their play.

Editing/Proofreading

Read your play. Use the checklist below to focus on the appearance of the script.

Conventions

☐ Did you use capitalization correctly, particularly with the names of characters and places?

☐ Did you use punctuation correctly, particularly after characters' names?

☐ Are there any spelling errors?

☐ Are the stage directions formatted correctly?

☐ Other **May include other questions about grammar, usage, and mechanics specific to play writing.**

Proofreading Marks

¶	Indent.
∧	Add something.
ℓ	Take something out.
∼	Transpose.
≡	Make a capital letter.
⊙	Add a period.

Publishing

Use this checklist to get your play ready to share.

Presentation

☐ Write your play on a clean sheet of paper. If possible, use a computer to type it.

☐ Check for any errors on your final copy.

☐ Make copies of your script for all the cast members and stage helpers. Have each character highlight his or her lines from the play. Have the stage helpers highlight what they need to do.

☐ Help cast members memorize their lines.

☐ Rehearse the play with the cast. Direct the cast members and stage helpers.

☐ Have the cast find costumes and props.

☐ Perform the play for your audience.

☐ Other **May include questions about presenting a play.**

Name _____ Date _____

Writing a Fantasy

Use the writing process to create a fantasy.

Prewriting

Who is the audience for your fantasy?

☐ Your friend

☐ Your teacher

☐ Your school newspaper

☐ Contest judges

☐ Other **Audience should be specific.** _____

What is your purpose for writing?

☐ To entertain the audience

☐ To make a point about something in the real world by using an imaginary situation

☐ To submit to a contest

☐ Other **Purpose should be clearly stated.** _____

Briefly describe the characters, setting, and plot of your fantasy.

Characters _____

Setting _____

Plot _____

_____

What elements of your fantasy could not be real?
Students may indicate talking animals and events that could not happen in the real world.

◀ **Writing a Fantasy**

Objective: Students plan the specific elements of their fantasy.

NARRATIVE WRITING

Expand your plan for your plot from the previous page using the story map. Plan a problem and resolution.

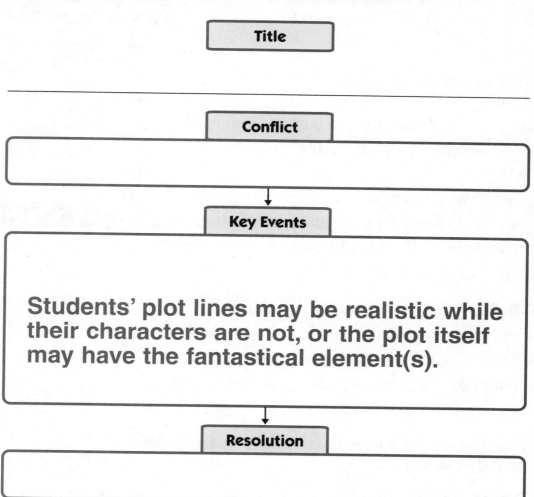

Title

Conflict

Key Events

Students' plot lines may be realistic while their characters are not, or the plot itself may have the fantastical element(s).

Resolution

Drafting

Write your fantasy on a sheet of paper using your plan.
▶ Include a beginning, middle, and end.
▶ Be sure to describe a problem and how it was solved.
▶ Describe the setting.
▶ You may want to describe the characters or slowly reveal them throughout the story.
▶ Use dialogue to help bring your characters to life.

UNIT 6 Journeys and Quests • **Lesson 4** *When Shlemiel Went to Warsaw*

Objective: Students revise their fantasy.

▶ **Writing a Fantasy**

Revising

Read your fantasy. Use this checklist to improve it. Use proofreading marks.

Ideas

☐ Does the beginning grab the audience's attention?

☐ Do parts of your story have a fantasy element?

☐ Do you give enough details about the characters and plot?

☐ Are your ideas original?

☐ Will your audience find your ideas interesting?

☐ Does your story have a problem or conflict that is solved?

☐ Is the plot suspenseful?

Organization

☐ Do the story events make sense and fit together?

☐ Are all the details ordered correctly?

☐ Does your story have a beginning, middle, and end?

Voice

☐ Will your audience be able to tell that you are interested in telling this story?

Word Choice

☐ Did you use precise words to describe the actions and characters?

☐ Do your words give your fantasy a certain mood?

Sentence Fluency

☐ Are your sentences smooth and easy to read?

☐ Other **May include specific questions related to writing a fantasy.**

Mark your corrections on your paper. If you have made many changes, write a revision.

Proofreading Marks

¶	Indent.
∧	Add something.
ℓ	Take something out.
∼	Transpose.
⌢sp⌢	Check spelling.
⊙	Add a period.

► **Writing a Fantasy**

Editing/Proofreading

Proofread your fantasy. Use the checklist below to make sure you remember everything. Use proofreading marks to make the changes.

Conventions

☐ Did you use the correct spelling, including personal names?

☐ Does each sentence have the correct punctuation?

☐ Did you use quotations with dialogue correctly?

☐ Have you written the correct form of comparative and superlative adjectives and adverbs?

☐ Other **May include other questions about grammar, usage, and mechanics.**

Proofreading Marks	
¶	Indent.
∧	Add something.
ℓ	Take something out.
∼	Transpose.
≡	Make a capital letter.
⊙	Add a period.

Publishing

Use this checklist to get your fantasy ready for publishing.

Presentation

☐ Rewrite your fantasy onto a clean sheet of paper, or type it on a computer.

☐ Read your fantasy for any final errors.

☐ If you wish, illustrate your fantasy.

☐ Present your fantasy by using one of the following methods.

► Read it to your audience.
► Send it to a magazine that publishes student writing.
► Give it to the editor of the school newspaper.
► Make a book out of it.
► Place it in your Writing Portfolio.

NARRATIVE WRITING

Objective: Students plan the audience and purpose for an adventure story.

UNIT 6 Journeys and Quests • **Lesson 5** *The Search*

Writing an Adventure

Prewriting

Who is the audience for your adventure?

☐ Your friend

☐ Your teacher

☐ Your school newspaper

☐ Contest judges

☐ Other **Audience should be specific.** _____

What is your purpose for writing?

☐ To entertain the audience

☐ To make the audience want to have an exciting adventure like the one in the story

☐ To imagine yourself living an exciting life

☐ To submit to a contest

☐ Other **Purpose should be clearly stated.** _____

Briefly describe the characters, setting, and plot of your adventure. Remember that these must seem like they could be real.

Characters _____

Setting _____

Plot **Students' setting may determine part of the plot.** _____

_____

_____

UNIT 6 Journeys and Quests • **Lesson 5** *The Search*

▶ Writing an Adventure

Objective: Students organize their ideas for an adventure story.

Expand your plan for the plot by using the story map.

Title

Conflict

Key Events

Students may need to do research to come up with realistic details for their adventure stories. The events of the plot must seem like they could be real.

Resolution

Drafting

Using the story map and other notes, write a draft of your adventure story. Focus on making your elements suspenseful and interesting. Don't forget the action verbs and colorful adjectives. Develop your characters and tell about their struggles. Your story should have a beginning, middle, and end.

Objective: Students revise their adventure story.

UNIT 6 Journeys and Quests • **Lesson 5** *The Search*

▶ **Writing an Adventure**

Revising

Reread your story. Use this checklist to improve it. Use proofreading marks to make changes.

Proofreading Marks

¶	Indent.
∧	Add something.
ℓ	Take something out.
∼	Transpose.
sp	Check spelling.
⊙	Add a period.

Ideas

☐ Did the actions in the story build suspense?

☐ Is your story original?

☐ Do you give enough detail to tell about the characters' struggles?

☐ Does the adventure seem like it could really happen?

☐ Does your opening catch the reader's interest?

Organization

☐ Do you have a beginning, middle, and end?

☐ Are events ordered in a way that will create the most suspense?

Voice

☐ Does your writing show your excitement for the story?

Word Choice

☐ Did you use action verbs and colorful adjectives?

Sentence Fluency

☐ Do the sentences flow from one to the next?

☐ Other **May include specific questions related to an adventure story.**

Make your changes on your paper. If you have made many changes, rewrite your adventure story.

UNIT 6 Journeys and Quests • **Lesson 5** *The Search*

▶ **Writing an Adventure**

Editing/Proofreading

Proofread your adventure story. Use this checklist to make sure you remember everything.

Conventions

☐ Did you use the correct spelling, including personal names and places?

☐ Does each sentence have the correct punctuation, including commas after introductory words and phrases?

☐ Did you use quotations with dialogue correctly?

☐ Other **May include other questions about grammar, usage, and mechanics.**

Publishing

Use this checklist to get your adventure ready for publishing.

Presentation

☐ Rewrite your adventure onto a clean sheet of paper, or type it on a computer.

☐ Read your story for any final errors.

☐ If you wish, illustrate your adventure story.

☐ Add anything else to make it visually appealing.

☐ Present your adventure by using one of the following methods.

   ▶ Read it to your audience.
   ▶ Send it to a magazine that publishes student writing.
   ▶ Give it to the editor of the school newspaper.
   ▶ Place it in your Writing Portfolio.
   ▶ Give a copy to a friend.
   ▶ With your class, make a book of all the adventure stories written in class.
   ▶ Give a copy to your school library or media center to include in a place for student writing.

Objective: Students edit and publish their adventure story.

NARRATIVE WRITING

Writing Historical Fiction

Objective: Students plan the audience and purpose for historical fiction.

Use the writing process to write a historical fiction story.

Prewriting

Who is the audience for the historical fiction?

☐ Your friend

☐ Your teacher

☐ Your school newspaper

☐ Contest judges

☐ Other **Audience should be specific.**

What is your purpose for writing?

☐ To entertain the audience

☐ To help the audience understand the events of a time period

☐ To educate about a person in history

☐ To tell about a way of life long ago

☐ To make the audience wish they could go back in time

☐ Other **Purpose should be clearly stated.**

Briefly describe the characters, setting, and plot of your historical fiction. Remember that these must seem like they could be real.

Characters _____

Setting _____

Plot **The struggle should fit with the time period.**

NARRATIVE WRITING

Objective: Students plan their ideas for historical fiction.

▶ **Writing Historical Fiction**

Plan your piece of historical fiction by expanding your ideas. You might have to do research for the details.

Title

Conflict

Key Events

Students' events should be relevant to the time period they chose.

Resolution

Drafting

Write your story on a sheet of paper.
▶ Decide on a narrator for the story and what point of view you will use.
▶ Describe the historical time and place.
▶ Work interesting background information into your story. Details should be accurate for the time period.
▶ List characters with details. Remember they should act the way people of the time acted.
▶ Try to create a feeling of suspense.

UNIT 6 Journeys and Quests • **Lesson 6** *Alberic the Wise*

Objective: Students revise their historical fiction story.

Revising

▶ **Writing Historical Fiction**

Reread your story. Use this checklist to improve it.

Ideas

☐ Are the events of the story interesting?

☐ Does the story build in interest and suspense?

☐ Do your details, characters, and actions fit the time period?

☐ Are your characters believable?

☐ Does the story have conflict and resolution?

Proofreading Marks

¶	Indent.
∧	Add something.
ℯ	Take something out.
⌣	Transpose.
sp⊘	Check spelling.
⊙	Add a period.

Organization

☐ Are the events told in a logical order?

☐ Have you used the same point of view throughout the story?

☐ Does your story have a beginning, middle, and end?

Voice

☐ Does your writing style involve the reader?

☐ Does your writing show your excitement for your topic?

Word Choice

☐ Do the characters' words make sense considering the historical time?

☐ Do your words describe the time and place accurately and vividly?

☐ Will the reader understand the words you used?

Sentence Fluency

☐ Do the sentences have a rhythm?

☐ Other __May include specific questions related to the__ __genre of historical fiction.__

Make your changes to your story.

UNIT 6 Journeys and Quests • **Lesson 6** *Alberic the Wise*

Editing/Proofreading

Proofread your story. Use this checklist to make sure you remember everything.

Conventions

☐ Did you use the correct spelling, including personal names and places?

☐ Does each sentence have the correct punctuation?

☐ Did you capitalize the names of historical events, characters, and other proper nouns?

☐ Did you use quotations with dialogue correctly?

☐ Do all your subjects agree with your verbs?

☐ Other __**May include other questions about grammar,**__ **usage, and mechanics.**

Publishing

Use this checklist to get your story ready to share.

Presentation

☐ Rewrite your story onto a clean sheet of paper, or type it on a computer.

☐ Check your story for any final errors.

☐ If you wish, illustrate your story with historical photos or illustrations.

☐ Present your story by using one of the following methods.

▶ Read it to your audience.
▶ Send it to a magazine that publishes student writing.
▶ Give it to the editor of the school newspaper.
▶ Place it in your Writing Portfolio.
▶ Give a copy to a friend.
▶ With your class, make a book of all the stories.
▶ Give a copy to your school library or media center to include in a place for student writing.

NARRATIVE WRITING

Cumulative Checklists

Ideas

☐ Is your main idea clear and focused? Is it interesting?

☐ Does your introduction state your main idea?

☐ Are any important ideas left out?

☐ Are any not-so-important ideas left in?

☐ Are your ideas appropriate for your audience?

☐ Do you present your main idea in an interesting way, especially in the introductory paragraph?

☐ Are your ideas accurate and, if necessary, supported by research?

☐ Have you included enough supporting details or examples to fully explain your main idea?

☐ Are the details you use specific and vivid?

☐ Does your conclusion leave the reader with something to think about, such as a new and interesting fact or quote?

Organization

☐ Are supporting details ordered in the most logical way?

☐ Have you organized your essay in a way that makes the most sense based on the idea you have chosen?

☐ Would a different organizational strategy be more effective? Would it appeal more to your audience?

☐ Did you include an introductory paragraph and a concluding paragraph that explain your main idea in an appealing or thought-provoking way?

☐ Do you include strong transitions to move the reader smoothly from one paragraph to the next?

☐ Do you include topic sentences to introduce new ideas?

☐ Does every main idea have at least two supporting ideas?

☐ Can you combine any smaller paragraphs or separate larger ones?

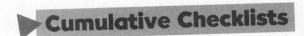

Revising

Word Choice

☐ Have you defined any words you think your audience will not understand?

☐ Are your nouns and verbs exact?

☐ Are your adjectives and adverbs vivid?

☐ Have you used your own words and phrases when summarizing information from another text?

☐ Do you use place and location and time and order words to help the reader understand where and when events take place?

☐ Have you taken care to choose just the right word to convey your meaning?

Sentence Fluency

☐ Does each sentence introduce a new idea or new piece of information?

☐ Have you avoided repeating what has already been said?

☐ Have you used transition words to move smoothly from one subject to another?

☐ Have you used different kinds and lengths of sentences to add variety to your writing?

☐ Have you used transition words and phrases to link sentences?

☐ Have you used conjunctions to combine short, choppy sentences?

Voice

☐ Do you sound confident, knowledgeable, and enthusiastic about your subject?

☐ Does the voice you use reflect the purpose of your writing?

☐ Have you confidently stated your opinion when appropriate?

☐ Does your writing sound like you?

REVISING CHECKLIST

Editing/Proofreading

Unit 1 Grammar and Usage

Lesson 1 ☐ Common and Proper Nouns

Lesson 2 ☐ Pronouns

Lesson 3 ☐ Action, State-of-Being, Linking, and Auxiliary Verbs

Lesson 4 ☐ Kinds of Sentences (Declarative, Interrogative, Imperative, and Exclamatory)

Lesson 5 ☐ Simple and Complete Subjects and Predicates and Sentence Fragments

Unit 2 Mechanics

Lesson 1 ☐ Capitalization of Places, Dates, Holidays, and People's Titles

Lesson 2 ☐ Capitalization of Proper Adjectives; Titles of Books, Movies, Magazines, and Newspapers; Historic Events; and Religions, Languages, and Ethnic Backgrounds

Lesson 3 ☐ Abbreviations

Lesson 4 ☐ Commas in Addresses, Names of Places, and Dates

Lesson 5 ☐ Parentheses, Hyphens, Dashes, and Ellipses

Lesson 6 ☐ Quotation Marks, Apostrophes, and Underlining

Unit 3 Grammar and Usage

Lesson 1 ☐ Adjectives

Lesson 2 ☐ Adverbs

Lesson 3 ☐ Prepositions

Lesson 4 ☐ Conjunctions and Interjections

Lesson 5 ☐ Possessive, Reflexive, Intensive, and Indefinite Pronouns

Editing/Proofreading

EDITING CHECKLIST

Unit 4 Grammar and Usage

Lesson 1 ☐ Types of Sentences (Simple, Compound, Complex)

Lesson 2 ☐ Subject-Verb Agreement

Lesson 3 ☐ Misused Words

Lesson 4 ☐ Comparative and Superlative Adjectives and Adverbs

Lesson 5 ☐ Direct and Indirect Objects

Lesson 6 ☐ Contractions, Negatives, and Double Negatives

Unit 5 Grammar, Usage, and Mechanics

Lesson 1 ☐ Fragments

Lesson 2 ☐ Commas with Introductory Phrases

Lesson 3 ☐ Punctuation and Capitalization in Friendly Letters

Lesson 4 ☐ Punctuation and Capitalization in Business Letters

Lesson 5 ☐ Commas with Independent and Subordinate Clauses

Lesson 6 ☐ Commas with Quotation Marks, Appositives, Interrupters, and Introductory Words

Publishing

Unit 2 Expository Writing

☐ Did you add diagrams or pictures to help explain your writing, if needed?

☐ If you have different sections in your writing, did you add headings that will stand out?

☐ Have you checked to make sure the finished product is visually appealing?

☐ Did you prepare a title page and bibliography if they are required?

Unit 3 Descriptive Writing and Poetry

☐ Did you read your final paper to check for errors in spelling or grammar?

☐ Have you used drawings, photos, or computer graphics to illustrate your writing?

☐ Did you add any charts or graphs that are needed to show any data you may have included?

☐ Have you presented your descriptive writing by using one of the following methods?

    Submitting it to a science or writing magazine

    Presenting it to your class

    Submitting it as part of a science fair project

☐ Have you presented your poem by using one of the following methods?

    Placing it in a collection of class poetry

    Placing it in your Writing Portfolio

    Mailing it to a magazine for a contest

    Sharing your poem by performing it

    Posting your work on a poetry Web site for young people

Publishing

Unit 4 Persuasive Writing

☐ For posters, flyers, and advertisements, have you added design and illustration elements to make them more visually appealing?

☐ When writing letters, have you checked to make sure you have done the following?

> Signed your letter
>
> Addressed the envelope
>
> Proofread the envelope and your letter one more time
>
> Mailed your letter with the correct postage

Unit 5 Personal Writing

☐ When writing letters have you made certain to do the following?

> Sign your letter
>
> Address and proofread the envelope. Put the person's name and title on the envelope.
>
> Fold the letter and place it in the envelope. Put the correct postage on the envelope and mail it.

Unit 6 Narrative Writing

☐ Did you present your writing by using one of the following methods?

> Putting your story into a book format
>
> Giving an oral presentation
>
> Publishing your writing electronically

☐ When writing a play, have you done the following?

> Made copies of your script for all the cast members and stage helpers
>
> Helped cast members memorize their lines
>
> Rehearsed the play with the cast
>
> Had the cast find costumes and props
>
> Performed the play for your audience

PUBLISHING CHECKLIST

Writer's Self Check

As strange as it may seem, the better a writer is, the *harder* he or she works at writing. The best writers are not the best because they are naturally talented. They are the best usually because they work the hardest. Good writers really do take *more* time than others in the planning and revising stages of the writing process.

Anyone can become a good writer, but it takes work. On the following pages are some of the things that good writers do.

- ☐ Listen to advice about time requirements and plan time accordingly.
- ☐ Spend time choosing, thinking about, and planning the topic.
- ☐ Spend time narrowing the topic.
- ☐ Consider the audience and what readers already know about the topic.
- ☐ Conduct research, if necessary, before writing.
- ☐ Get information from a lot of different sources.
- ☐ Use models for different types of writing, but develop individual plans.
- ☐ Organize the resource information.
- ☐ Make a plan for writing that shows how the ideas will be organized.

Famous Writers on Writing

"No tears in the writer, no tears in the reader. No surprise in the writer, no surprise in the reader."

—Robert Frost,
Pulitzer Prize-winning poet

"In writing, as in life, the connections of all sorts of relationships and kinds lie in wait of discovery, and give out their signals to the Geiger counter of the charged imagination, once it is drawn into the right field."

—Eudora Welty,

1973 Pulitzer Prize for Fiction,
author of *The Optimist's Daughter*

Drafting

☐ Express all ideas in the first draft.

☐ Stop and think about what is being written while drafting.

☐ Evaluate and alter ideas while drafting.

☐ Change or elaborate on original plans while drafting.

Famous Writers on Writing

"Only a mediocre writer is always at his best."

—Somerset Maugham,
author of *Of Human Bondage*

"As in all my books for a long time the problem was structure. I never start writing until I've sorted that out."

—Gabriel Garcia Marquez,

1982 Nobel Prize for Literature,
author of *One Hundred Years of Solitude*

"If I didn't know the ending of a story, I wouldn't begin. I always write my last line, my last paragraph, my last page first."

—Katherine Anne Porter,

1966 Pulitzer Prize for Fiction,
author of *Ship of Fools*

"I have to write about something that I myself am interested in and that I want to learn more about."

—Russel Freedman,

author of *Lincoln: A Photobiograhpy*

"I have never thought of myself as a good writer. Anyone who wants reassurance of that should read one of my first drafts. But I'm one of the world's great rewriters.

—James A. Michener,

1948 Pulitzer Prize for Fiction,
author of *Tales of the South Pacific*

Revising

☐ Look back and evaluate what has been written.

☐ Read the draft repeatedly as a reader, not the writer.

☐ Identify problems in the draft.

☐ Think of solutions to problems and understand when solutions will and won't work.

☐ Recognize when and how the text needs to be reorganized.

☐ Eliminate sentences or paragraphs that don't fit the main idea.

☐ Identify ideas that need elaboration.

☐ Do more research if needed to support or add ideas.

☐ Identify and eliminate unnecessary details.

☐ Ask for feedback from peer and teacher conferences.

☐ Take advantage of classroom and outside resources.

☐ Check the accuracy of facts and details.

☐ Give credit for any ideas from other people or sources.

☐ Present and support personal points of view and ideas.

Famous Writers on Writing

"The point of good writing is knowing when to stop."

—L.M. Montgomery,
author of *Anne of Green Gables*

"The task of a writer consists of being able to make something out of an idea."

—Thomas Mann,

1929 Nobel Laureate in Literature,
author of *The Magic Mountain*

SELF CHECK

- ☐ Edit the work to allow the reader to understand and enjoy the words.
- ☐ Correct most errors in English language conventions.
- ☐ Use resources or seek assistance to address any uncertainties in English language conventions.

Publishing

- ☐ Present the work in a way that makes it easy to read and understand.
- ☐ Consider format, style, illustration, as well as clarity in the presentation of the work.
- ☐ Show pride in the finished work.

Famous Writers on Writing

"The beautiful part of writing is that you don't have to get it right the first time, unlike, say, a brain surgeon. You can always do it better, find the exact word, the apt phrase, the leaping simile. With each novel, I fill a shopping bag with material that has been rewritten"

—Robert Cormier,
author of *I am the Cheese*

"There is no great writing, only great rewriting."

—Justice Louis D. Brandeis, Associate
Justice of the U.S. Supreme Court

"Writing, the art of communicating thoughts to the mind through the eye, is the great invention of the world . . . enabling us to converse with the dead, the absent, and the unborn, at all distances of time and space."

—Abraham Lincoln

While Spider-Man struggles with criminals, criminal mayors, loneliness without Mary Jane by his side and disturbing nightmares of a gruesome bandaged mystery apparently named Kindred, he's been unaware of another foreboding development. Kindred has summoned to their side a man Spider-Man knows to be dead. A man who's since observed the criminal activities of several old familiar malefactors and might have brought down brutal retribution on some of them. In life, this man was sometimes called Stanley Carter, but he also had another name.

the AMAZING SPIDER-MAN

SINS RISING

WRITER **NICK SPENCER**

AMAZING SPIDER-MAN: SINS RISING PRELUDE

ARTIST	**GUILLERMO SANNA**
COLOR ARTIST	**JORDIE BELLAIRE**
COVER ART	**RYAN OTTLEY & NATHAN FAIRBAIRN**

AMAZING SPIDER-MAN #44

ARTIST	**KIM JACINTO** WITH **BRUNO OLIVEIRA**
COLOR ARTIST	**DAVID CURIEL**
COVER ART	**CARLOS GÓMEZ & MORRY HOLLOWELL**

AMAZING SPIDER-MAN #45

PENCILER	**MARK BAGLEY**
INKERS	**JOHN DELL** WITH **ANDY OWENS**
COLOR ARTIST	**DAVID CURIEL**
COVER ART	**CASANOVAS**

AMAZING SPIDER-MAN #46-47

PENCILER	**MARCELO FERREIRA**
INKERS	**ROBERTO POGGI**
COLOR ARTIST	**DAVID CURIEL**
COVER ART	**CASANOVAS**

VC's **JOE CARAMAGNA**
LETTERER

TOM GRONEMAN
ASSISTANT EDITOR

KATHLEEN WISNESKI
ASSOCIATE EDITOR

NICK LOWE
EDITOR

SPIDER-MAN CREATED BY STAN LEE & STEVE DITKO

COLLECTION EDITOR **JENNIFER GRÜNWALD**
ASSISTANT MANAGING EDITOR **MAIA LOY** ❀ ASSISTANT MANAGING EDITOR **LISA MONTALBANO**
EDITOR, SPECIAL PROJECTS **MARK D. BEAZLEY** ❀ VP PRODUCTION & SPECIAL PROJECTS **JEFF YOUNGQUIST**
BOOK DESIGNERS **ADAM DEL RE** with **JAY BOWEN**
SVP PRINT, SALES & MARKETING **DAVID GABRIEL** ❀ EDITOR IN CHIEF **C.B. CEBULSKI**

SINS RISING PRELUDE VARIANT BY BOSSLOGIC

SINS RISING PRELUDE

--TO A LITTLE BACKWATER DEEP IN THE *OZARK* MOUNTAINS--

--TO BE RAISED BY MY PATERNAL *GRANDPARENTS.*

MY GRANDFATHER WAS A HARD, ANGRY MAN WHO PREACHED *HELLFIRE* AND *BRIMSTONE* TO ABOUT A DOZEN PENTECOSTALS EVERY SUNDAY.

HE REVILED HIS ONLY SON FOR SPURNING HIS FAITH AND RUNNING AWAY TO SODOM TO DANCE WITH THE HEATHENS, ONLY TO DIE A DRUGGIE--

--AND THERE I WAS, THE *REMINDER* OF IT ALL.

IF HE COULDN'T PUNISH HIS SON FOR HIS TRANSGRESSIONS--

--HE WOULD PUNISH *ME* INSTEAD.

JUST LIKE HIM, AREN'T YOU, BOY? SOFT.

THE TRUTH IS, I DIDN'T FEEL ANYTHING WHEN I KILLED IT.

JUST LIKE I DIDN'T FEEL ANYTHING WHEN A RATTLER BIT INTO MY GRANDFATHER DURING THE SNAKE HANDLING AT A TENT REVIVAL.

MY GRANDMOTHER AND THE REST OF THE CONGREGATION, ON THE OTHER HAND, FELT *PLENTY.* NO ONE COULD UNDERSTAND HOW THE MOST RIGHTEOUS MAN THEY KNEW HAD BEEN TAKEN THIS WAY.

THE HOLY SPIRIT WAS SUPPOSED TO *PROTECT* HIM, KEEP HIM CLEANSED OF SIN. UNLESS HE *WASN'T,* SOMEHOW.

AND SO, BEING THE SUPERSTITIOUS BUNCH THEY WERE, THEY DECIDED TO MAKE SURE THEIR PREACHER MADE IT TO HEAVEN--

AND SOON ENOUGH, WHEN ALL ELSE HAD GONE DARK AND QUIET, *HE* CAME--

--BUT *I* HAD TO SEE.

--BY CALLING ON SOMETHING I'D ONLY HEARD ABOUT IN WHISPERS.

SOMETHING TERRIBLE AND DECIDEDLY *UNHOLY.* THEY LAID HIS BODY OUT OVERNIGHT, THEN LOCKED THEMSELVES AWAY--

--THE *SIN EATER.*

THEY'D EXISTED AS LONG AS ANYONE COULD REMEMBER-- GOING BACK TO THE OLD COUNTRY--BUT NEVER MORE THAN ONE AT A TIME.

HERMITS WHO HID OUT IN THE WOODS UNTIL THEY WERE CALLED UPON TO PERFORM THEIR RITUAL.

THE FAMILY SET A MEAL ON THEIR DEAD LOVED ONE'S CHEST--AN OFFERING REPRESENTING THE DECEASED'S SINS.

THE SIN EATER CONSUMED IT, TOOK THOSE TRANSGRESSIONS AS HIS OWN. ALLOWING THE SPIRIT TO ASCEND.

YOU WOULD THINK THAT SACRIFICE WOULD MERIT THEM SOME KINDNESS OR RESPECT, BUT NO. THEY WERE SHUNNED AND HATED.

IF THEY DARED SHOW THEIR FACES IN PUBLIC, NO ONE LOOKED THEM IN THE EYE. TO THE FAMILIES, THEY REPRESENTED HIDDEN SHAMES AND SECRETS. BUT I SAW SOMETHING ELSE.

AFTER ALL, WHAT WAS I BUT ANOTHER MAN'S SINS MADE FLESH?

SOMETHING I RECOGNIZED.

I CARRIED THE BURDEN OF WHAT MY FATHER HAD DONE AND HAD PAID THE PRICE FOR IT.

BUT IF I WAS PREPARED FOR WHAT I SAW, I DEFINITELY WASN'T PREPARED--

DETECTIVE CARTER--

--DO YOU HAVE A MOMENT?

I JUST WANTED TO MAKE SURE YOU WERE OKAY.

I APPRECIATE YOUR CONCERN, FATHER--BUT THIS... THIS ISN'T WHAT I SHOULD BE DOING RIGHT NOW.

YOU MEAN THERE'S SOMETHING MORE *IMPORTANT* RIGHT NOW THAN LAYING YOUR PARTNER TO REST AND PAYING YOUR RESPECT?

YES.

GETTING HIM SOME *JUSTICE.*

HNN. I *UNDERSTAND.*

YOU KNOW, WHEN I WAS AN ALTAR BOY, I TOOK MONEY FROM THE COLLECTION. NOT MUCH, BUT MY FAMILY--WE DIDN'T HAVE MEANS, AND I WAS A KID.

I WANTED TO *LIVE* A LITTLE. I'D TAKE IT AND I'D BUY BASEBALL CARDS AND BUBBLEGUM.

NOT SURE I FOLLOW.

I NEVER GOT CAUGHT, YOU SEE.

AS FAR AS EVERYONE ELSE WAS CONCERNED, I WAS THE MOST DEVOTED, TRUSTWORTHY ALTAR BOY YOU COULD ASK FOR. I KNEW EXACTLY HOW TO HIDE THE GUILT ON MY FACE--

SO NOW I KNEW WHO THE *LEAD INVESTIGATOR* WAS.

JEAN, WHY DID YOU HAVE TO *LIE* TO ME?

BUT THE *GOOD NEWS* IS NOW I HAVE EVERYTHING I NEED TO FIND OUT WHAT REALLY HAPPENED--

--RIGHT AT MY FINGERTIPS.

SO THEY DO HAVE A SUSPECT. A TIP FROM AN INFORMANT PROVIDES A NAME.

BUT HIS RECORDS ARE SEALED--

--WHICH MEANS I'LL NEED A COURT ORDER.

NYPD! OPEN UP!

WHAT THE HELL IS THIS?! WHO DO YOU--

JUDGE ROSENTHAL. GOOD EVENING.

DETECTIVE CARTER? WHAT--WHAT THE DEVIL ARE YOU DOING HERE?! DO YOU HAVE ANY IDEA HOW INAPPROPRIATE THIS IS?

I DO. I NEED A FAVOR.

NOW?! ARE YOU OUT OF YOUR MIND?! IT'S TWO IN THE MORNING!

IT CERTAINLY IS, JUDGE--

--YOUR WIFE MUST BE WORRIED SICK ABOUT YOU.

SOFT.

THERE IS POWER IN FORGIVENESS!

ELEVATOR GO UP... ELEVATOR GO DOWN...

--LET'S GIVE A WARM ROUND OF APPLAUSE FOR OUR GUEST TONIGHT--

--DETECTIVE STANLEY CARTER!

CLAP CLAP

CLAP CLAP CLAP

CLAP CLAP

CLAP CLAP

THERE WE ARE-- HAVE A SEAT.

SO, STAN... THERE'S NO GOOD WAY TO ASK THIS, BUT... WHAT'S IT *LIKE* BEING A *MASS MURDERER?*

YOU ALREADY ASKED ME THAT...

I--I--I'VE BEEN HERE BEFORE.

WELL, YOU SURE HAVE. PLENTY OF TIMES. BUT THIS TIME YOU'VE GOT SOMETHING *EXTRA-SPECIAL* TO SHOW US, DON'T YOU?

I... D-DO I?

I UNDERSTAND WE HAVE A CLIP. YOU WANT TO SET IT UP FOR THE FOLKS OUT THERE?

IT--IT W-W-WAS ME...

HOLD THE POPGUN, TORK.

I GOT HIM DRENCHED, WRAPPED IN INSULATION AND WEBBED-UP. HE SHOULDN'T BE A PROBLEM.

OH, NO.

STAN!

CARTER, YOU FOOL! WHAT HAVE YOU DONE?

WHAT HAVE YOU DONE?!!

STAN, WHAT HAVE YOU DONE?

I'VE... WON, SIN-EATER D-DEAD.

NOW I CAN LIVE...

HE WAS SO FAR GONE... HE THOUGHT SIN-EATER AND HE WERE TWO DIFFERENT PEOPLE.

IN THAT CASE.

CARTER HAD THE LAST LAUGH.

HE NEVER LOADED SIN-EATER'S GUN.

NEXT

DON'T MISS THE PULSATING RETURN OF ONE OF SPIDER-MAN'S DEADLIEST FOES--

THE TARANTULA!!

BE THERE!

YOU SEE, STAN?

YOU REALLY HAD A WONDERFUL LIFE. DON'T YOU SEE WHAT A MISTAKE IT WOULD BE--

--TO JUST THROW IT AWAY?

NOT WHEN I CAN HELP YOU FULFILL YOUR DESTINY. YOUR CALLING.

I CAN RETURN YOU TO THE WORLD THAT SCORNED YOU--

I CAN HELP YOU CLEANSE THEM ALL. ALL YOU GOTTA DO IS ACCEPT IT.

AH, THERE HE IS...MY CHAMPION--

44

BEWARE THE RISING

CAN I JUST SAY HOW *NICE* IT'S BEEN LATELY?

YOU AND ME. JUST THE TWO OF US--

--NOBODY ELSE AROUND TO GET IN THE WAY.

BECAUSE I HAVE *SO MUCH* I WANT TO SHOW YOU, *PETE.*

THERE'S SO MUCH FOR US TO TALK ABOUT.

AND SURE, I'M HOPEFUL--EXCITED, EVEN--ABOUT US MEETING FACE-TO-FACE.

BUT FOR NOW, LET'S JUST *ENJOY* THIS.

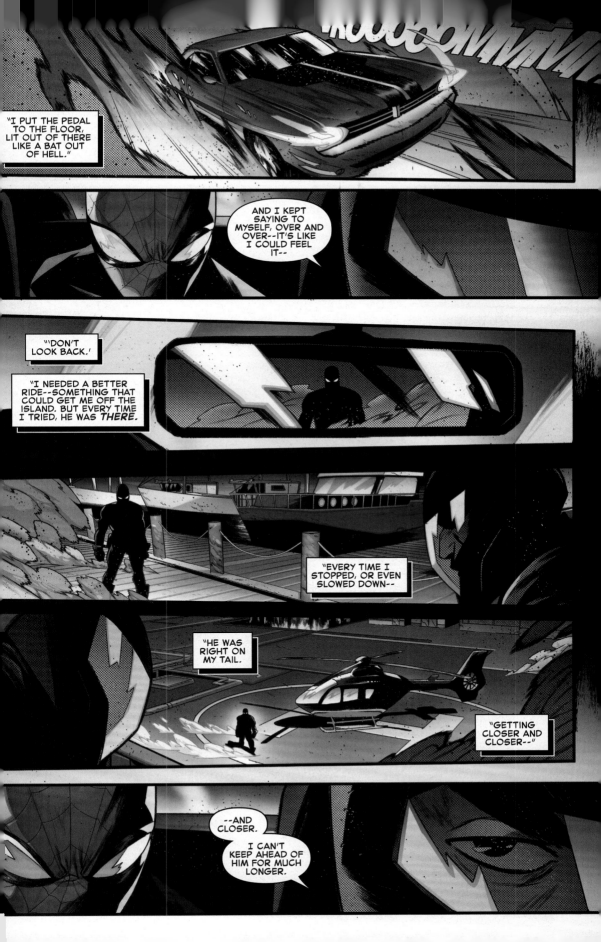

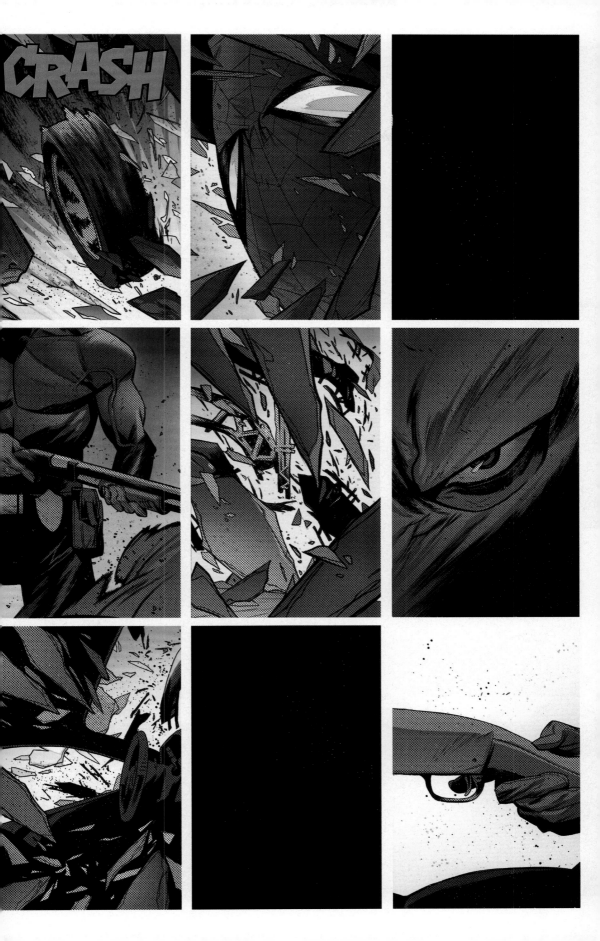

--I'M NOT SURE *I'M* OKAY.

I'M NOT SLEEPING GREAT. AND EVEN WHEN I'M AWAKE, THINGS JUST FEEL... WRONG.

THEY HAVE EVER SINCE--

--EVER SINCE YOU LEFT.

DON'T GET ME WRONG. I'M GLAD YOU WENT--

OR NOT *GLAD,* BUT-- YOU KNOW WHAT I MEAN. I'M HAPPY YOU GOT THIS CHANCE. I WANNA SUPPORT YOU HOWEVER I CAN.

"IT'S JUST--THAT NIGHT I SHOWED UP AT YOUR PLACE, AFTER MYSTERIO ATTACKED WITH THAT FAKE ALIEN INVASION? I MEANT WHAT I SAID--

"--IT'S GETTING HARDER TO DO THIS WITHOUT YOU."

THE OTHER DAY I DID THIS...PODCAST WITH JONAH. DON'T ASK.

HE SAID SOME STUFF THAT KINDA HIT HOME. OKAY, SURE, IT'S *JONAH,* SO IT WASN'T TOTALLY ACCURATE, BUT HE WAS TALKING ABOUT HOW I KEEP PEOPLE AT A DISTANCE.

HOW I PRETEND IT'S BECAUSE I DON'T WANT THEM TO GET HURT--

--BUT THE TRUTH IS MORE *COMPLICATED* THAN THAT.

THERE WAS THIS TIME, AFTER WE BROKE UP, I'D GOTTEN IN SUPER LATE FROM PATROL, AND JUST CRASHED--PASSED OUT AS SOON AS I GOT THROUGH THE WINDOW.

THE NEXT MORNING, I WOKE UP, RUNNING LATE LIKE ALWAYS, SO I THREW ON SOME CLOTHES AND WENT TO RUN OUT THE DOOR, AND I ALMOST DIDN'T CATCH IT 'TIL I WAS OUTSIDE.

I STILL HAD MY *MASK* ON.

IT DIDN'T HAPPEN ALL AT ONCE. BUT JUST, AS TIME WENT ON, THE HOURS I WAS SPIDER-MAN KEPT GOING UP. THE HOURS I WAS JUST PETER PARKER KEPT GOING DOWN.

I TELL MYSELF, HEY, MAYBE IT'S BETTER THIS WAY. PEOPLE ARE COUNTING ON ME, THIS IS MORE IMPORTANT. IT'S ALWAYS GONNA BE MORE IMPORTANT THAN, I DUNNO...

GROCERY SHOPPING. READING A BOOK. GOING FOR A WALK.

I AM SO AFRAID IT'S GONNA SWALLOW ME WHOLE.

"I HAVE TO PUT THE MASK ON. I KNOW THAT. OTHERWISE, PEOPLE DIE. I HAVE A *RESPONSIBILITY.*"

"BUT I *NEED* YOU, MJ."

THIS THING I DO, IT JUST... IT TAKES AND TAKES AND TAKES. AND I AM SO AFRAID...

I NEED A REASON TO TAKE THE MASK OFF.

EY, I'M SORRY, I KNOW THAT'S KINDA AVY. LIKE I SAID, I--I HAVEN'T BEEN EEPING WELL. AND HONESTLY, I'M JUST AMAZED YOUR VOICE MAIL HASN'T CUT ME OFF.

I GUESS JUST--THERE WAS THIS THING I WANTED TO ASK YOU BEFORE YOU LEFT. I MEAN, BEFORE I MESSED EVERYTHING UP AND MISSED YOU LEAVING. YOU KNOW WHAT? NEVER MIND--

--WE CAN TALK ABOUT IT WHEN YOU GET BACK.

I LOVE YOU. TALK TO YOU S--

TING

45

SINS RISING PART 1

LIFE MOVED PRETTY FAST FROM THERE.

I MET A GUY, FELL IN LOVE. THINGS SEEMED PRETTY GREAT...

UNTIL I LEARNED THE GUY WAS ACTUALLY *THE AMAZING SPIDER-MAN* OF ALL PEOPLE. AND BELIEVE IT OR NOT, THAT WASN'T THE BIGGEST SURPRISE I GOT.

NO, THAT HAD TO BE LEARNING THAT MY DEARLY DEPARTED DAD WASN'T SO DEPARTED AFTER ALL.

WHEN I LEARNED HE'D FAKED HIS DEATH BECAUSE HE WAS IN CAHOOTS WITH THE MASKED CRIMINAL MYSTERIO. YEAH...

...TURNS OUT THE GUY WASN'T SUCH A HERO TO BEGIN WITH.

AFTER THAT, THINGS GOT...PRETTY DARK.

I WAS SINKING INTO THIS WORLD OF WEIRD COSTUMES AND POWERS. ONCE I HAD A NASTY RUN-IN WITH THE GOBLIN SERUM, I KNEW I'D HAD ENOUGH.

SO I LEFT. HEADED SOUTH.

I WONDER...WHY WAS I THINKING ABOUT *MY* LIFE JUST NOW?

GUESS I JUST GOT TIRED OF RUNNING. THE DEPARTMENT WAS WILLING TO GIVE ME MY JOB BACK--

--BUT I KNEW I NEEDED *MORE.*

I FOUND A SUPPORT GROUP FOR PEOPLE WHO OFTEN FOUND THEMSELVES ON THE COLLATERAL DAMAGE SIDE OF SUPER HERO BUSINESS--

--WHICH IN TURN LED TO STRIKING UP A CLOSE FRIENDSHIP WITH ANOTHER AMAZING SPIDER-EX (AND ONCE AGAIN CURRENT).

LIFE SLOWLY GOT BACK TO NORMAL.

WELL, AS NORMAL AS IT GETS FOR *ME,* I GUESS. AT THE VERY LEAST--

⤜SIGH⤛ LET'S SEE WHAT WE'VE GOT.

--HERE'S HOPING FOR NO MORE SURPRISES.

'TIS SWEET AND COMMENDABLE IN YOUR NATURE, HAMLET, TO GIVE THESE MOURNING DUTIES TO YOUR FATHER--

I HAVEN'T BEEN SLEEPING WELL LATELY.

IT'S THESE *DREAMS* I'VE BEEN HAVING. I CAN'T REALLY REMEMBER THEM. JUST *FLASHES.*

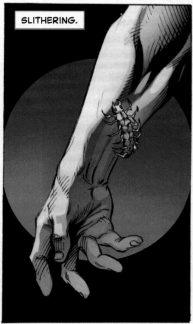

SLITHERING.

CRASHING.

SINKING.

YEAH, NOT VERY PLEASANT. I GOTTA ADMIT, THOUGH--

BUT YOU MUST KNOW YOUR FATHER LOST A FATHER; THAT FATHER LOST, LOST HIS--

--AND THE SURVIVOR BOUND IN FILIAL OBLIGATION FOR SOME TERM TO DO OBSEQUIOUS SORROW. BUT TO PERSEVERE--

--THIS IS HELPING.

AND I GET WHAT YOU'RE WONDERING--WHAT IS *PETER PARKER,* KNOWN DROWSER-OFFER DOING SOAKING UP SOME *SHAKESPEARE IN THE PARK* ON A FRIDAY EVENING? WELL--

--I WASN'T SUPPOSED TO BE ALONE.

THERE WAS A *PLAN*.

MJ WAS SUPPOSED TO BE BACK IN TOWN, HYPING UP HER NEW MOVIE.

SO I MADE A RESERVATION AT THE BEST RESTAURANT IN TOWN, WHERE I WOULD PRETEND TO KNOW WHAT I WAS ORDERING--

--AND THEN I WAS GONNA TAKE HER *HERE*. HER *FAVORITE*. SHAKESPEARE IN THE PARK.

YEAH, YEAH, I KNOW-- GREAT PLAN, PARKER.

BUT THAT WASN'T THE BEST PART. NO, THE BEST PART--

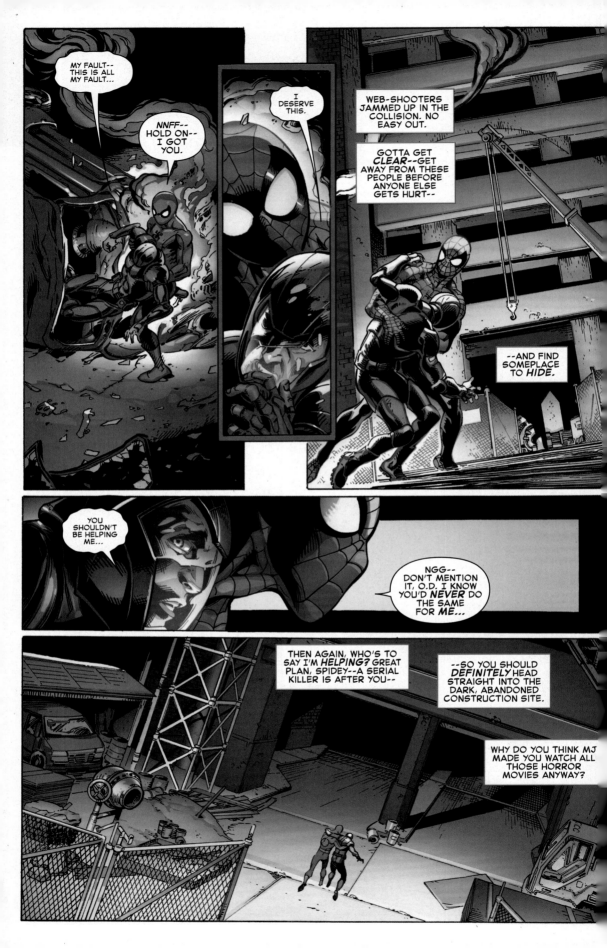

I NEVER EVEN *WANTED* TO BE A BAD GUY, YOU KNOW THAT? WANTED TO BE--

--WANTED TO BE LIKE *YOU*.

YEAH? WELL, TRUST ME, BUDDY, IT'S A LITTLE *OVERRATED*.

THIS ISN'T GONNA *WORK*. NOT GONNA GET AWAY FROM THIS GUY. GOTTA FACE HIM HEAD-ON.

I JUST NEEDED THE *MONEY*...

YOU STAY RIGHT HERE, OKAY? STAY LOW, DON'T MOVE.

SPIDEY, PLEASE... YOU GOTTA BELIEVE ME.

I DIDN'T WANT ANYONE TO GET HURT.

OH MAN, OVERDRIVE...

WHAT THE HECK DID YOU GET YOURSELF INTO?

YOU SHOULD GIVE HIM TO ME, SPIDER-MAN.

I KEEP WANTING TO BELIEVE IT ISN'T HIM.

WITH ALL THE BAD GUYS PASSING THROUGH THE REVOLVING DOOR OF DEATH, I'LL ADMIT I WAS REALLY HOPING *HIS* WOULD STICK.

THE
SIN-
EATER.

THE MASKED
PSYCHOPATH
WHO MURDERED
JEAN DEWOLFF
AND TWO OTHER
INNOCENT
PEOPLE.

HE WAS ACTUALLY
STAN CARTER, A
POLICE DETECTIVE WHO
FOOLED EVERYONE--
INCLUDING ME.

HIS RAMPAGE
NEARLY TOOK THE
LIFE OF MY GOOD
FRIEND BETTY
BRANT.

THAT SENT ME INTO
A RAGE. I HONESTLY
THINK I MIGHT'VE
CROSSED THE LINE
WITH THIS GUY--

--UNTIL DAREDEVIL
STOPPED ME.

AFTER HE WAS INSTITUTIONALIZED, STAN WAS TREATED AND RELEASED.

THE DOCTORS SAID HE WAS NO LONGER A THREAT TO ANYONE.

I DIDN'T BELIEVE IT. I WAS STILL SO ANGRY. SO I WENT AND *CONFRONTED* HIM.

IT DIDN'T GO WELL.

NOT LONG AFTER, HE--HE TOOK HIS OWN LIFE.

HE BAITED THE POLICE INTO SHOOTING HIM, BUT THE TRUTH IS, I'VE ALWAYS FELT AT LEAST *PARTLY* RESPONSIBLE.

IT'S SOMETHING I'VE TRIED TO *BURY.* BUT NOW IT'S AT THE FRONT OF MY MIND, *SCREAMING* AT ME.

STUPID.

SLOWING ME DOWN.

...HAT'S ALL YOU *WANT* TO SEE. DO WHAT I AM *COMMANDED* TO DO! I *ALWAYS* HAVE! YET STILL YOU CALL ME *STANLEY*-- THE LUNATIC, THE *COP KILLER.*

AND YET HERE *YOU* ARE, PROTECTING THE DRIVER, WHEN HIS SINS ARE SO MUCH *WORSE!*

NFFF-- WHAT ARE YOU TALKING ABOUT?

WHY DON'T YOU ASK *HIM?!*

ASK HIM ABOUT THE *NINE DEAD* POLICEMEN AND -WOMEN! ASK HIM ABOUT THE *CHILDREN* WHO LOST THEIR *FAMILIES!*

WAIT--THE POLICE KILLINGS ON THE LOWER EAST SIDE THAT WERE ALL OVER THE NEWS?

NOBODY HAD ANY LEADS, BUT IT COULDN'T HAVE BEEN...

LOOK, *CARTER*-- WHATEVER IT IS OVERDRIVE HAS DONE, HE'S GIVEN UP. HE'LL FACE A *JURY*, NOT *YOU.*

HH. NOW WHO'S THE *FOOL?*

HE'LL NEVER FACE JUSTICE. HE'S A *COWARD.* HE WON'T EVER TRY TO REPENT.

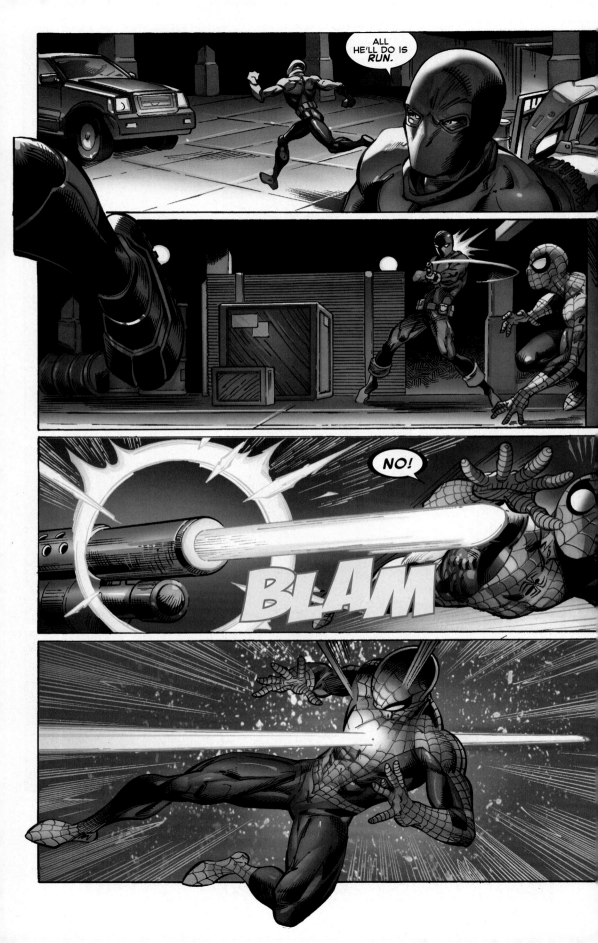

AND NOW I'M GUESSING YOU WANNA DO *ME* A KINDNESS, TOO.

NO. YOU'LL FACE YOUR SINS, BUT NOT WITH *ME*.

THE ONE WHO CALLED ME, THE ONE WHO...

HE HAS A *PLAN* FOR YOU, TOO.

I'M JUST HERE TO MAKE READY THE PATH.

I'LL SEE YOU SOON, SPIDER-MAN.

THE WORK IS NOT YET DONE.

"NOT YET DONE."

THE WORDS KEEP CRAWLING AROUND IN MY HEAD.

I DON'T KNOW WHAT CARTER WANTS--OR WHERE HE'LL TURN UP NEXT. BUT I CAN ALREADY TELL--

--THINGS ARE ONLY GOING TO GET WORSE FROM HERE.

I NEED TO WAKE UP. SNAP OUT OF THIS FOG I'VE BEEN IN.

BECAUSE I CAN'T SHAKE THE FEELING, AWFUL AS THIS IS--

--THAT SOMETHING ELSE IS LURKING BEHIND ALL OF THIS.

STOP LOOKING OVER YOUR SHOULDER, SPIDEY.

THE SIN-EATER IS BACK. AND WHEREVER HE GOES--

--DEATH FOLLOWS.

JAMES BEVERLEY-- AFRICAN AMERICAN MALE, AGE THIRTY- TWO--CAUSE OF DEATH, GUNSHOT WOUND TO THE CHEST.

ONE SMALL PROBLEM THERE...

THE WOUND IS... GONE.

I DON'T KNOW HOW TO EXPLAIN IT. WHEN HE WAS BROUGHT IN, IT WAS STILL THERE. I SAW IT MYSELF.

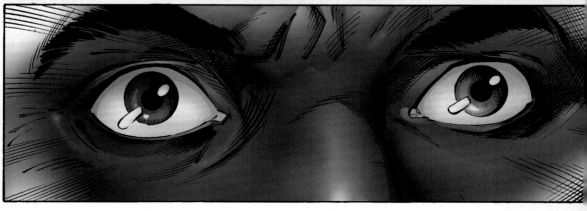

AHHHHH!

W-W-WHAT HAPPENED TO ME?!

46

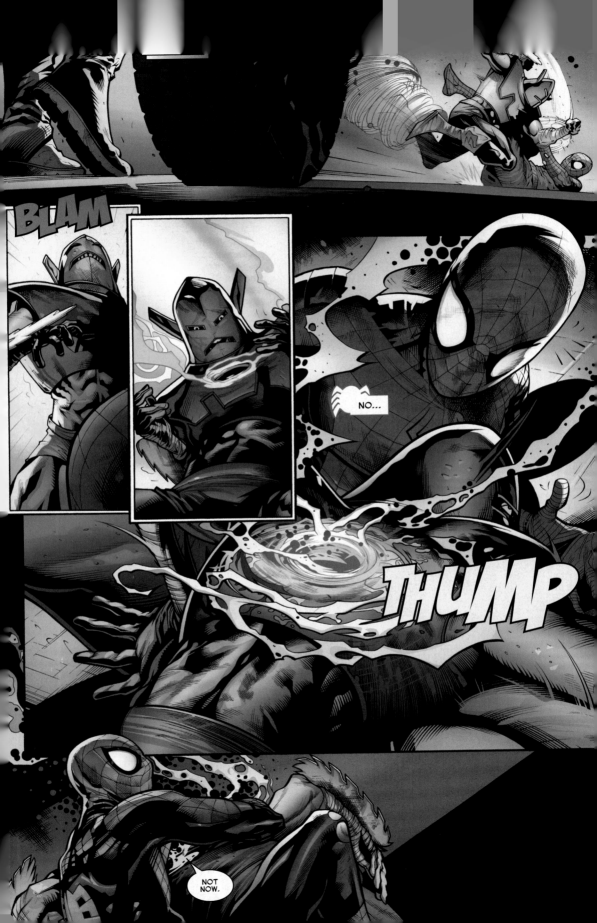

THIS IS *RORY MATTHIESON.* HE WAS--HE WAS MY BEST FRIEND. HE LOVED THIS STUFF. SCIENCE.

HE BEGGED ME TO COME TO THIS THING. AND WHEN THEY BUSTED IN, HE TRIED TO SHIELD ME, AND THE GUY WITH THE BUZZ SAWS, HE--

AND YOU'RE SERIOUSLY ASKING ME WHY I *APPLAUDED?*

SARAH CRAWLEY, BARTENDER.

AM I *ASHAMED* THAT I DID? I DON'T KNOW. PERHAPS A FEW YEARS AGO, I WOULD'VE BEEN.

BUT THESE ARE DANGEROUS, DANGEROUS TIMES.

AN WESTMEYER, MINISTRATOR.

DUDE WAS *AWESOME,* YOU ASK ME. HE'S LIKE THE *PUNISHER,* RIGHT?

BUT THE PUNISHER'S A *REGULAR GUY.* THIS ONE CAN ACTUALLY GET THE JOB DONE.

JON PORTER, STUDENT.

AN'T STOP THINKING ABOUT IT. MEAN, I GET *SOME* OF IT. IT'S T LIKE I HAVEN'T--WELL, LOOK, METIMES MY ANGER'S GOTTEN HE BETTER OF ME, AND I'VE ANTED TO SEE SOMEBODY-- YOU KNOW.

BUT TO *CHEER* FOR IT? TO CLAP? WHEN YOU SEE SOMEONE *BRUTALLY MURDERED?* THEN AGAIN--

--WE BOTH KNOW IT'S MORE *COMPLICATED* THAN THAT, DON'T WE?

I BEEN AN E.M.T. FOR SEVENTEEN YEARS. I'VE SEEN SOME CRAZY THINGS.

AND I SEEN MORE BODIES THAN I KNOW HOW TO COUNT. SO WHEN I TELL YOU THOSE CLOWNS WERE DEAD--

HERB RODRIGUEZ, E.M.T.

"--I MEAN THEY WERE *DEAD*. POINT-BLANK SHOTGUN WOUNDS WILL DO THAT. HELL, HALF THE NEFARIOUS GUY'S HEAD WAS MISSING.

"THEY WOULDN'T LET US IN 'TIL THEY GOT THE MACHINE QUIETED DOWN--BUT SOON AS WE DID, AS SOON AS I GOT TO THE BODY--

"--THE BODY GOT RIGHT BACK UP."

NOW LOOK, I GET IT, THE WORLD'S A DIFFERENT PLACE FOR THESE TYPES. THEY'RE ALWAYS DEAD, THEN ALIVE AGAIN, THEN DEAD AGAIN, THEN--

THAT I CAN FOLLOW. BUT THAT'S NOT THE CRAZY PART.

P-P-PLEASE-- IS EVERYONE ALL RIGHT?

"IS EVERYONE ALL RIGHT?"

AN HOUR BEFO THE GUY WAS *STONE-COLD KI* BUT THE SECON CAME BACK, HE HARMLESS AS A P YOU EVER HEAR SOMETHIN' LIK THAT?

NO--

--NO, I HAVEN'T.

I'LL BE HONEST, MS. WINTERS. I TRIED TO FIGHT HAVING THEM SENT HERE. I THOUGHT THEY BELONGED ON THE RAFT OR SOME BLACK SITE.

BUT THE TRUTH IS, THEY'VE BEEN LIKE THIS EVER SINCE THEY WERE ADMITTED--

--MODEL PATIENTS.

ALL DUE RESPECT, BUT THIS IS *RAVENCROFT*. MODEL PATIENT USUALLY MEANS THEY ONLY KILLED THREE ORDERLIES APIECE THIS WEEK.

SEE FOR YOURSELF.

RAVENCROFT.

"HEY SPEND MOST OF THEIR TIME QUIET, HUDDLED ONE TOGETHER.

"BUT WHEN THEY TAKE BREAKS FROM THAT, IT'S TO PERFORM RANDOM ACTS OF KINDNESS FOR THE OTHER PATIENTS.

"THEY HAVEN'T RAISED THEIR VOICES--LET ALONE THEIR FISTS--IN ANGER ONCE SINCE THEY GOT HERE.

"HELL, *WHIRLWIND* ENDED UP IN THE INFIRMARY AFTER SOME OLD ASSOCIATES PAID HIM A VISIT. HE DIDN'T EVEN TRY TO DEFEND HIMSELF.

"DOES THAT SOUND LIKE HIS FILE?"

I NEED TO TALK TO THEM.

NOT A CHANCE. THESE PEOPLE ARE IN TREATMENT. WE HAVE *PROTOCOLS*, YOU KNOW--

NONSENSE, DOCTOR--

47

SINS RISING PART 3

THREATS &
MENACES OFFICE.

UNION SQUARE.

I GUESS I SHOULDN'T BE SURPRISED.

AM I THE FIRST ONE HERE?

HH--

DOWN AND AROUND THE BACK. MAKE SURE YOU'VE GOT THAT ON.

CARLIE'S RIGHT.

I WANT TO BELIEVE THEY'VE BEEN *BRAINWASHED*. THAT HE'S USED SOM OCCULT POWER TO LURE THEM HERE.

THE UNCOMFORTABLE REALITY IS HE'S OFFERING THEM A CHANCE TO IMPOSE THEIR WILL ON OTHERS--

A CHANCE TO *HURT* OTHERS--

WHICH, YEAH--

OHHHH OOSSSSSHHH

--IS EASIER SAID THAN DONE.

ON HIS OWN, I CAN HANDLE THE SIN-EATER IN A FAIR FIGHT.

BUT NOW-- AFTER HE "CLEANSED" THE LETHAL LEGION AND TOOK THEIR POWERS--

NNNNNZZZZRP

--IT'S A WHOLE DIFFERENT BALL GAME.

FWOO

WATCH NOW, ALL OF YOU.

KRP

SOON YOU WILL BE ABLE TO DO ALL OF THIS AND MORE.

"--SEE WHAT YOUR SINS HAVE DONE."

HE'S COMING!

THUD

KSSSH

KRAK

BRRRRRAAAAAHHH!

HE'S COMING FOR YOU!

DO YOU HEAR HIS MESSAGE?

#44 MARVEL ZOMBIES VARIANT BY
TONY DANIEL & FRANK D'ARMATA

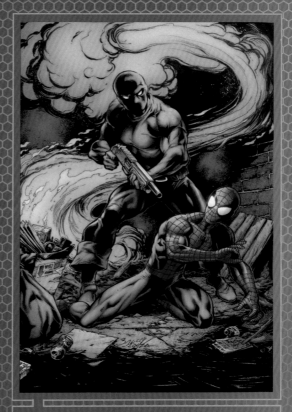

#45 VARIANT BY
MARK BAGLEY, JOHN DELL & MORRY HOLLOWELL

#46 VARIANT BY
MARK BAGLEY, JOHN DELL & MORRY HOLLOWELL

#47 VARIANT BY MARK BAGLEY, JOHN DELL & JASON KEITH